The Red Sea Mission team has always been a favourite of mine – simply because I knew the founder so well. The first time we met was when I was a student in Glasgow in 1954. Today I still remember the message he gave from 2 Kings 2:19-22. Little did I know that we would become close friends, and that working in Open Doors I would have so much contact with him. Many times Lionel and I shared the platform at conferences, imparting the vision for the Muslim world. Reading this book was great; I came across so many familiar names and places. Please read it, and if you do you will not be able to forget the courage of these men and women who took the message of Jesus to Islam. I hope there will be more books about this great mission.

Brother Andrew

This account of the way in which God called, led and intervened in the life of his servants in the Red Sea Mission Team will teach and inspire open-minded Christians to trust the same all-sufficient God in the generations yet to come.

James Nyquist

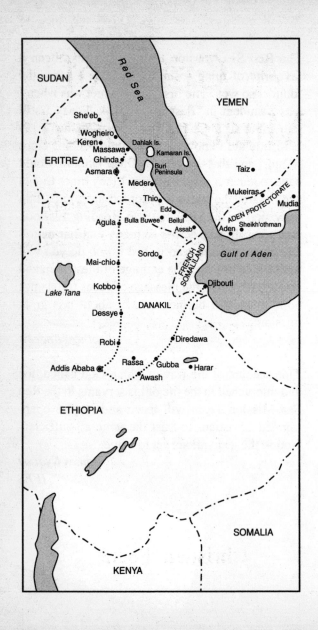

A Grain of Mustard Seed

The story of the origins of the Red Sea Mission Team

Bevan Woodhead

Christian Focus

ISBN 1 85792 398 7

Published in 1998 by
Christian Focus Publications
Geanies House, Fearn, Ross-shire
IV20 1 TW, Great Britain

Cover design by Donna Macleod

CONTENTS

Christian Focus Publications publishes biblically-accurate books for adults and children. The books in the adult range are published in three imprints.

Mentor focuses on books written at a level suitable for Bible College and seminary students, pastors, and others; the imprint includes commentaries, doctrinal studies, examination of current issues, and church history.

Christian Heritage contains classic writings from the past.

Christian Focus contains popular works including biographies, commentaries, doctrine, and Christian living.

For a free catalogue of all our titles, please write to
Christian Focus Publications,
Geanies House, Fearn,
Ross-shire, IV20 1TW, Great Britain

For details of our titles visit us on our web site
http://www.christianfocus.com

PREFACE

Reading this record has not only humbled me and left me full of praise to our God, it has filled me in on many details of which I was sadly ignorant. My mother, now with Christ some twenty years, knew Bevan and Lionel long before I did. She was heavily committed to their pioneer labours for the Lord. As you will see, Mother sent out some of the early prayer letters, and sent up many fervent prayers on behalf of these intrepid servants of the Lord. Though married to a part-Jewish husband who had come to believe firmly in the Lord Jesus as his own personal Saviour, Mother shared a great burden for the Arab world as well as for the Jewish world.

It was in Nazareth in 1981 that I was first fully aware of meeting Bevan and Elna in the Edinburgh Medical Mission Hospital. I had the great privilege of preaching from the Carpenter's Bench-shaped pulpit. Later I heard about the great work being done in Israeli Universities by John, the student son of Bevan and Elna. The existence of the Evangelical Christian Unions bringing together Jewish and Arab Bible-believing students was largely due to John's efforts and prayers. Had I anticipated this, I would have made more of an effort to meet Bevan and his family at an earlier date. How often we are only wise after the event!

The details in this book will be precious to all connected with the Red Sea Mission Team, especially those whose first thoughts about becoming a foreign missionary were triggered off by Lionel Gurney's confrontation question, as those blue eyes of his pierced your innermost being: 'Why aren't you on the mission field?' This single-eyed doctor cum-statesman cum-teacher cum-leader accomplished much in his recently fulfilled life of over eighty years. Bevan, the doctor's intimate friend and colleague, comes through very clearly in these pages. Not surprising, as his diary for the period provides most of the facts narrated. He was there!

I warmly commend this fascinating paperback to your reading and your prayers.

Leith Samuel
Frinton-on-Sea

It was a great privilege for me to live through those very precious first five and a half years of the founding of the Team. It is clear that the calling of this band of Christ's disciples together, for the task of reaching the unevangelized tribes of the Red Sea Area, and the wider challenge of the Muslim World, is an outworking of his 'Unchanging Commission'. He promises to be always with his disciples, and his presence was, and is, very evident, unfolding his plan – guiding, ruling and overruling – the Team.

During those years I kept very full diaries; actually it is the only time in my life I have done so consistently. When asked, years later, to provide material for a possible future book, the diaries along with various events that were burned into my memory enabled me to do so. I have been able to present some of the picture in this book, but I hope more of the amazing dealings of God will be written by other members of the Team.

Bevan Woodhead, the author of this book,
went to be with the Lord on 31st July, 1996.

1

The First Beginning, a Grain of Mustard Seed

Lionel Gurney, who was to be the Lord's instrument in founding the Red Sea Mission Team, qualified in medicine at Bristol University in 1934. His aim was to make surgery his career, but the Lord had other plans for his life.

Alfred Buxton, who had gone out to Belgian Congo with C.T. Studd, later worked in Abyssinia (Ethiopia) with the Bible Churchman's Missionary Society (BCMS). In 1934 he came to Britain to challenge young people to work in Abyssinia, hoping to recruit eighteen of them. One of those challenged, and who responded, was his distant cousin, Lionel Gurney. Lionel went out with Alfred in September 1934, but he was asked initially to help in the Church of Scotland Mission Hospital in Aden for seven months as a locum. This was Lionel's introduction to work among Muslims.

When he rejoined Alfred in Ethiopia, Lionel found that there were a number of missions working there, and many churches established by them. He felt strongly that he should go to where Christ was not known. Alfred shared Lionel's concern and told him of the Danakil tribe (also called Afar), an unreached, fanatically Muslim tribe with an unwritten language. They lived in an area which was part of that assigned to BCMS, but the mission did not have any missionaries available to pioneer the area. Eventually,

Lionel was able to help in an area of the Danakil where a malaria epidemic was raging. Later he spent six months, with another missionary, learning the Danakil language.

Meanwhile, the Italians had invaded Ethiopia, and it was not long before the missionaries were expelled. It was while in Danakil that the Lord showed Lionel that his call was to the needy Muslim world. The Lord gave him a wonderful promise from Genesis 28:15 – that he would not forsake him and would bring him back again into the land. I had the privilege of accompanying Lionel twenty years later, when the Lord faithfully fulfilled this promise.

After being expelled from Abyssinia, Lionel was able to work for a time among many Abyssinian refugees in British Somaliland.[1] Then he managed to get a free trip back to Britain on a British warship.

After World War II started, a plan was drawn up to drive the Italians out of Ethiopia and reinstate Haile Selassie, at that time in exile in Britain, as Emperor. Lionel and David Stokes, a dear friend he had worked with in BCMS, were both conversant in Amharic, the language of Ethiopia, and well acquainted with the country and culture. They were appointed to be members of a team to accompany the Emperor.

Lionel returned to Britain when the assignment was accomplished, and took the Diploma in Tropical Medicine at Liverpool. This, too, was an important part of his preparation.

---

1. Later, this was a substantial factor in our obtaining acceptance to open up the Red Sea Mission Team work in Ethiopia, and in Eritrea, which had become federated to Ethiopia.

When the war ended, BCMS was able to re-open the work in Ethiopia, with David Stokes as Field Leader. Meanwhile Lionel was carrying out evangelistic work in the Addis Ababa area, since he had not yet been given permission to enter into Danakil. He gathered together an evangelism team of Ethiopian believers, mostly graduates of BCMS Bible School. The Lord greatly blessed their witness, especially to prison inmates (more about this later).

These Ethiopian believers did not receive a salary, therefore Lionel in a gesture of solidarity renounced his salary without them knowing. Despite periods of testings, the Lord honoured his faith and supplied his needs. This, too, was essential in the Lord's preparation of Lionel to found the Red Sea Mission Team.

Lionel believed that the Lord wanted him to pioneer a work for Muslims, particularly in the Red Sea region. Consequently he resigned from BCMS, and the way opened up for him to serve again in the Church of Scotland Hospital in Aden. He worked as Protectorate Medical Officer for a year.

Burdened to travel around Britain, Canada and the USA to challenge young Christians, Lionel was hindered by a lack of finance. The Lord was again teaching him important lessons. On return to Britain, Lionel received a letter from a senior mission leader of SIM, inviting him to the USA and Canada for a speaking tour, to share the needs of those in the Red Sea area. I believe this played a vital role in raising up prayer warriors and stewards of God to fulfil the vision the Lord had given Lionel.

However Lionel returned to Britain deeply

disappointed, for he had expected hundreds of young people to respond. It seemed he would have to meet the challenge alone.

God's call to me

I had qualified as an analytical chemist and as a gas engineer. During the war I had volunteered to join the RAF to train as a pilot. However, the first atomic bomb was dropped just a week after we got our 'wings'. Although a churchgoer, I was quite an unbeliever. To me, the Bible was merely a collection of legends, interspersed with ancient history, but scarcely relevant to our present day.

Back in industry from the RAF, I came up against the power of Satan in a terrifying way. I was trying to fight evil in my own strength, whilst denying Satan's very existence. Indeed I resembled the man who built his house on the sand: in the storm everything came crashing down; my life was in ruins. Abandoning his subtle disguise, Satan confronted me, presenting his way as the only way out. At first, I surrendered. But five days later, in his mercy, God instilled his fear in me, by making plain to me where Satan's way would lead. On my knees I cried out to God – whose existence I nevertheless still doubted – from my heart, beseeching him to help me. I told him I wanted the way of truth and righteousness, not the way of evil. I neither saw nor heard anything, but later I was conscious of a change within. For the first time, at the age of 33, I knew that the Bible was the inspired Word of God. I began reading it, starting at Genesis, believing every word.

Three months later, having read half of the Old Testament, I found the Lord Jesus Christ as my Saviour, or rather was found by him. He lifted me out of a horrible pit, out of the miry clay, and set my feet upon a Rock and established my goings. It was such a tremendous deliverance, and the realization came that I was redeemed by his paying the penalty for my sins on the Cross.

In appreciation of this priceless gift, I told my heavenly Father that I wished to give him my life, my body, my future, all that I possessed, so that others too would come to receive his salvation. I knew that my thank offering had been accepted, for I became conscious of the Holy Spirit arranging situations, leading, guiding, teaching and equipping me for his purposes.

He outlined to me the places to which I should go: Wales, England, Scotland and Ireland; then I would go to Jerusalem and other parts of the world, before finishing in Israel. Between 1947 to 1949 the Lord had fulfilled the first part. I then worked in my own profession while waiting on him to show me the next step. I contemplated going to a Bible School, and had applied to one for September 1951. Stepping out in faith, I gave three months notice to my employer, thus allowing him time to find a replacement.

A very dear friend, Mrs. J.K. Samuel, the mother of Leith Samuel, sent out Dr. Gurney's prayer letters. When she heard that I would be at the Keswick Convention in July 1951, she wrote that I should contact Dr. Gurney who would also be there.

Keswick Convention, 1951

When I introduced myself to Dr. Gurney, he immediately challenged me to go with him to South Arabia. I said that God had called me to the Jews, but promised to pray about it. This I did. Nevertheless I did not sense that it was not of the Lord.

Hence I was quite shaken when I was confronted with 'Arabia' in different ways. Although the Bible College said I could start in September, the Lord showed me very clearly that I had to go to another of his schools, 'The Backside of the Desert.' I was quite elated. Although the Lord showed me that there would be periods of severe testing and breaking, I was convinced that that was where he wanted me to go. Indeed I had a deep peace as I gladly assented. The Lord made it evident to me that this was to prepare me for Israel, and would be the door by which I would enter that land.

Before getting to bed on that Sunday evening, I remembered that at Keswick I had bought the second volume of the life of Hudson Taylor. The first thing I saw on opening the book was, 'Part 1 – The Backside of the Desert.' I got on my knees and poured out my heart in thanksgiving to the Lord for directing me so clearly.

A week later I wrote to Lionel. He replied that it was a call to Islam for the rest of my days. I had no peace about that, and wrote that the call was indeed of God, but it was to be God's school to fit me for Israel. If he would accept me on those terms I would gladly join him. He wrote back, exclaiming, 'Praise the Lord, welcome!'

He also informed me that Dr. Bernard Walker of the Church of Scotland Mission in Aden had cabled enquiring whether Lionel could take on the medical work in the Abyan area of the Aden Protectorate for at least one year. Lionel agreed to do so for twelve months, requesting permission at the same time to take a friend, Bevan Woodhead. Dr. Walker cabled back, 'Welcome, and bring your friend. Come as soon as possible.'

In a letter to Dr. Gurney I asked him if he would mind travelling directly to Aden, whilst I would trek out via Jerusalem. He appealed to me not to do this for the Lord's sake, and the Lord gave me peace about it.

The start of 'The Team'

Despite being a polio victim, Miss Gypsie Perkins had served in India for a number of years as private secretary to Dr. Brown, the founder of the Ludhiana Mission Hospital. She wrote to Dr. Gurney stating that the Lord had laid on her heart to look after the home end of his work. He replied that he did not have a work, and there was no home end to oversee. However she persisted, asserting that the Lord was pressing her in the matter.

In Chichester, Jack Budd arranged an open air meeting for Dr. Gurney to address. At the close a missionary challenge was given and the Lord laid it upon Jack to join us. Later, Kath, Jack's wife, was given confirmation that it was of the Lord. They had two young boys, Ray and Mike, aged about seven and five respectively.

On 19th September 1951, I left for Angmering to join Lionel. Lionel's 80-year-old mother, who had been a missionary in Japan, was also there. Because much shipping had been sunk, there were no passages to Aden until February 1952. Lionel, however, discovered that he could book a passage on the *Champollion*, due to sail from Marseilles to Beirut, via Alexandria and Port Said, in October 1951.

Lionel arranged for Miss Perkins and Jack Budd to come to Angmering on 9th October. And so it was that we were able to welcome our first secretary to administer home affairs and our first missionary, just prior to our departure to Aden. My diary entry for that day reflected my amazement at God's meticulous orchestration of events: 'Wonderful to see God's plan unfolding.'

2

The Journey out to Aden

Lionel had written to ask Keith Stevenson in Baghdad (Near East and Arabian Mission) if he could meet the boat in Beirut, and Keith had agreed.

We left London for Marseilles on Saturday, 13th October. On the way, Lionel spoke to a student meeting at Beattenberg Bible College in Switzerland. Through him the Lord called two of the students to serve him among Muslims. One was Bruno Herm who later joined us in Aden. The other was his brother, Daniel, who went out later with the Afghan Border Crusade.

We left Marseilles on 20th October on the *Champollion*. At our table for meals was Moshe, a young Jew from Alexandria with whom I had some good spiritual talks. When he disembarked in Alexandria, a Jewish lady was assigned to his place. The Lord was not letting me forget my call.

At Beirut Keith Stevenson was on the quay to meet us. This was Friday, and he shouted up that he had to be in Jerusalem by Monday night. Lionel had not intended to go to Jerusalem, but I was amazed to see the Lord fulfilling meticulously the plan he had revealed to me.

In Beirut we met Abu Marouf, the father-in-law of Dr. Affara of the Church of Scotland Hospital in Aden. He informed us that his son, Marouf, with his family, were soon to fly to Aden to stay, at the Lord's call. Lionel knew Marouf, and when he heard this he said, 'Bev, I believe the Lord is purposing to build his church in Aden, and is sending Marouf to be a pillar.' These were indeed prophetic words.

We then visited Roy Whitman in Amman. He had been a missionary for twenty-five years and had been wonderfully used by the Lord in all the surrounding countries. We crossed the Jordan and then went to Jerusalem. From there, through the barbed wire, we could see right across the land of Israel. Lionel was indeed surprised, as he had had no intention of going to Jerusalem.

After being with Marouf and family we returned to Roy because he was going to Baghdad and we were able to travel with him. He drove us to Irbid, where we stayed with Douglas and Mrs. Howells. The next day, with Roy, we started on our way for Baghdad in an old bone-shaker bus. Apart from a meal at a ramshackle restaurant, we travelled twenty-four hours non-stop across the Iraqi desert to Baghdad.

Keith had gone on ahead to Baghdad, and we stayed with him for three weeks. Daily we were in the streets of Baghdad, talking to people and distributing Scripture portions and tracts printed in Arabic. One young man asked where he could find out more. We gave him Keith's address, and he came that evening. Then each evening he returned bringing others with him, until between twenty and twenty-five Muslims were gathering to hear the Word of God. That young man had really come to faith in Christ and later he worked with Keith as an evangelist.

To Kuwait - unforgettable!

Our journey took us by train to Basra. In Basra we were advised to go to Kuwait to get a boat for Aden. This meant getting a bus from a village near Basra. It left whenever the driver thought there were enough passengers. The "bus!!?" was an old lorry with planks as seats. It left with a full load at 4 pm; we had waited since 7 am. After three hours the engine broke down, evidently a faulty ignition coil. The driver stopped a car and asked the occupants to take a message asking for another coil to be sent. While we were waiting for the coil to arrive, we offered to our fellow passengers a copy each of an Arabic Gospel. They were all Muslims and none accepted a copy. After three hours a taxi arrived with a coil. The diagnosis had been correct; the engine started, and we set off.

In the desert there were no roads as such, just tracks in the sand. Eventually we were all dozing. I awoke at about 1 am, to find that there were no tracks visible in the sand, and the driver was turning left for awhile, then to the right. Clearly he had lost his way. The sand got softer and he had to change to bottom gear. Eventually the bus stuck in the soft sand. All the passengers had to get out and help claw the sand from the wheels. We then had to push as the lorry moved off, scrambling aboard again while it was moving. This was repeated many times. Finally, when the driver started up, instead of the lorry moving forward, the wheels spun, sending a stream of sand shooting backwards. The rear of the lorry sank to its axle, with its nose pointing skywards. Any hope of shifting it this time had to be abandoned.

After some time Lionel said to me, 'Bev, the Muslims are usually fatalistic, but in this situation they are really worried. Here we are, lost in the desert without food or water. Tomorrow, in the heat of the sun, our situation will be rather desperate. I believe that we should tell them that we are going to pray to God, in the name of the Lord Jesus, to help us. Are you willing to stand with me in it?' My reply was a fervent 'Amen!'

He then explained to them in Arabic what he purposed to do. In the starlight, I could see some of them shrugging their shoulders. Lionel began to pray in Arabic, with one hand on my shoulder, and the other raised towards Heaven. While he was still praying, we heard, to our astonishment, a voice saying in English, 'Hello! What is the trouble?'

We opened our eyes to see two men approaching us out of the darkness. One of them introduced himself: 'My name is Teesdale, this is my friend Geordie.' Lionel replied, 'My name is Gurney, this is my friend Woodhead.'

Mr. Teesdale explained: 'We have an oil prospecting camp about a quarter of a mile away. I heard a lorry stopping, starting, and then a long silence. So I suspected it was in trouble. I woke Geordie, and we decided to come in the direction of the last sound I heard.'

Lionel said, 'Even if you have a hundred men, I doubt if you can do much about this lorry.'

'Oh! That's easy,' said Mr. Teesdale. 'We have six Dodge Power Wagons at the Camp, we will soon have you out.' He asked Geordie to go and bring one.

When Geordie returned, he attached a cable to our lorry and quickly and easily hauled it out of the sand. He then towed us about a mile and a half to the main tracks, and showed us our direction.

Within a short time, each of the passengers asked for an Arabic Gospel.[1]

At 3 am we arrived at the Kuwaiti Police and Customs Post. Soon, all those on duty, about nine, came asking for Gospels. They said they had heard what had happened to us in the desert.

We arrived in Kuwait, and managed to get a deck passage on a boat from there to Bahrain, from where we sailed to Aden, arriving there on Christmas Eve 1951. Dr. Walker had sent a Landrover to take us to Sheikh Othman, about ten miles around the bay. There was a Christmas party taking place in Dr. Affara's house and we had a really wonderful welcome. Marouf, Suad and family had already arrived and were among those to welcome us.

We were assigned to the Abyan area under Dr. Walker, the Protectorate Medical Officer. It was an agricultural area, irrigated by a system developed to

---

1. Some years later, I heard from Roy Whitman that many people had perished there in similar circumstances. At the time we were rejoicing in our wonderful, faithful God who can reach out to us in deliverance anywhere, when we cry out to him in the name of Jesus. What Lionel did not tell me was that, if there had been no deliverance, they would probably have slit our throats as they regarded us as infidels and the cause of the disaster. The Lord had put me in his school, 'The Backside of the Desert', to learn from a teacher of his choice: one who really believed in him and counted on his faithfulness, one who would obey him because he loved him, even to death.

use flash-flood waters from the mountains of Yemen to cultivate a 200 square mile area. Lionel was in charge of the anti-malarial spraying teams, built up by Dr. Walker, and about eight clinics, as well as all the public health and medical work in the area. They were really strenuous days. Very often Lionel would not come home until 7, 8, or even 9 pm, covered in sweat and dust, and worn out. After a short rest and a meal, there would be a meeting of enquirers, a Bible study for those showing a real interest in the gospel, as well as seeing more patients. Very often there were one, two or three calls for him during the night. Yet I never saw the sun rise that Lionel was not already on his knees before the Lord, or feasting on his Word.

The spiritual battles were fierce. Conversions in particular provoked counter-attacks from the enemy. At one stage I was prevented from working in the Protectorate. Yet in one sense, it was a very happy time for me, but for Lionel it was a time of very great pressure, even to breaking point.[2]

Meanwhile, Quardhy (Religious Judge) Mansoor

2. During this time Jack Budd wrote to say that he was coming out at the beginning of the hot season in 1952, so giving him time to get things ready for Kath and the children coming at the beginning of the cool season. Lionel was very worried as there was no opening for Jack, and no accommodation. Rev. Col. McGuffie was running a very fine Boys Club in Aden, and Lionel had heard that he was retiring. Lionel asked me to speak to Rev. Borch-Jensen, leader of the Danish Mission, to see if they would take over the Boys Club and to ask if Jack Budd may be able to help. Jack had had a lot of experience with young peoples' work. I met B-J, as he was known, at a prayer meeting. He said he wanted to speak to me about the Boys Club. They would be very sorry if such a good work

of Abyan was admitted to the hospital for an operation. He had been Minister for Education under Imam Abdullah, the previous ruler of the Yemen. However, under the tyrannical Imam Ahmed, he and his wife had to flee for their lives to the Aden Protectorate. As Religious Judge of the Lower Yaffa Tribe, he had become very interested in the Bible through Mustafa, a convert from Islam, who was one of Dr. Walker's medical dressers. When I spoke to the Quardhy I found that he had read the Bible six times. Almost daily we had long discussions on the Bible, and also on Luther, the Reformation, and Church history; he was indeed quite well read on these subjects.

One day he told me that he had just found out why I was not out in Abyan with Dr. Gurney. He said, 'I will be returning to Abyan soon and I will see that you will get back to be with Dr. Gurney.' He called a meeting of the Maglis (Council) and by sheer oratory persuaded them to unanimously invite me back to the Protectorate. When I went back, I was able to take Jack with me for a visit.

We heard later that the Governor of Aden had said that Woodhead must never be allowed in the Protectorate. However, the politicians could not do anything about it when the Arab Maglis had unanimously invited me back.

---

ceased. They had considered asking the Colonel if they could take it over, but they did not have anyone to run it. He said that he had heard Mr. Budd was soon coming out to join us, and if it could be arranged for Mr. Budd to run it, they would gladly take it on. He really was delighted when I told him of Lionel's request for me to speak to him on the very same lines. Jack arrived on May 6th, 1952, the Lord having sealed his call.

One of those who had very reluctantly agreed to my return was the Mensab, the religious Mayor of Ga'ar, the main town of the area, and where our clinic was. Quardhy Mansoor was quite an accomplished diplomat. He invited Dr. Gurney and me to supper, together with the Mensab. Having an Arab meal, squatting on the floor and eating with the hands, is very relaxing and conducive to good relationships. The Mensab was beginning to thaw, but then the Quardhy raised the question of Jesus and the gospel. Lionel said in no uncertain terms that Jesus Christ is the Son of the Living God, that he died on the Cross to pay for our sins, and would redeem us if we put our trust in him. The Mensab stiffened up, then stood and remained aloof, his face like thunder.

The Quardhy arranged cushions for us all to recline on, but the Mensab just sat on his heels with his back against the wall. We and the Quardhy reclined, and the Quardhy then tried to smooth things over with diplomacy. He spoke of how many of the people and incidents in the Old and New Testaments were also in the Koran. He asserted that there was very little difference between the Koran and the Bible. Lionel slapped his thigh and said, 'You are absolutely right! There is very little difference between night and day, it is only a matter of half an hour in the morning.' The Quardhy was just rocking with laughter, and the Mensab smiled and began to relax and recline on the cushions. Lionel loved the Muslims for the Lord's sake, and knew them very well. He knew they have quite a keen sense of humour and, no matter how grim the situation, once they start laughing the barriers in relationships melt. It was really heart warming. The next day the Mensab came to the clinic with a large water-melon for Dr. Gurney.

We were able to continue for some months, even though the spiritual battle continued to rage. There was a very subtle and dangerous attempt to eliminate the gospel witness, while retaining the medical work. Lionel knew that the Lord was showing him not to compromise, even if we were expelled from the Protectorate. The Lord showed that he knew the people had experienced his love and care, and even if we were expelled, the Mission would be invited back without restriction on the spiritual outreach. Lionel knew that even the missionaries may not understand if we were put out; we may even be ostracized. All this is exactly what happened.

During this time we were both getting clear leading from the Lord about the crossing of the Red Sea, and we both felt that the Lord was indicating Danakil.

Marion Thomas

While we could see the door closing in Abyan, Lionel had a letter from Marion Thomas to say that she believed God was calling her to join us. Marion was a very highly trained and qualified nurse and midwife. She had done one year of a two year course at Mount Hermon Bible College.

Lionel was continually challenging young Christians to offer their lives to the Lord for the mission fields, particularly for the Muslims. However, if any felt called to join us, he poured cold water on them. His reason for doing this was that he knew that if they were truly experiencing God's call, they would persevere. He really gave Marion a dose of cold water in his reply.

Marion took the letter to Gypsie Perkins, our Home Secretary, who agreed that it was a shaker. However, Marion said that, despite everything, she still believed that the Lord was calling her and had received confirmation even after getting Dr. Gurney's letter. Gypsie asked Marion if she was willing to join her in asking the Lord for a final seal if it was really of him. She said that Mrs. Budd and the boys were booked to sail to Aden, leaving in a few weeks' time. She added that in the natural sense the accommodation had long since been booked up, but they would ask the Lord that if he wanted Marion to go to Aden at that time, he would grant her a passage with the Budds. She would contact the ship's agents and let Marion know the result. Marion and another girl at the College spent all night in prayer. During the early hours of the morning the Lord gave them an assurance that the passage had been granted and they changed from praying to praising.

The agents said it had been completely booked up for some time, but would contact the shipping company. Gypsie rang Marion to tell her to keep praying. Marion's response was, 'We have finished praying for it, Perks; we are praising him instead, because he has shown us that he has granted the passage.' Later, Gypsie rang again to give the news from the shipping company that there was just one berth available, and it was for a lady.

When Marion went two weeks later to board the

boat with Kath and her two small boys, she found that they were in the same cabin. Obviously wonderfully arranged and sealed by the Lord.[3]

Meanwhile, circumstances led to Lionel and I having to leave the Protectorate.[4] Though we were subsequently asked to return, by that time the Lord had very clearly confirmed his leading to us for the Danakil Tribe.

---

3. Lionel's faith was very worried about accommodation for the Budd family. In fact, he had been thinking of writing to stop Kath coming, but the Lord graciously intervened. He used Karen Olsen of the Danish Mission to come to the rescue. Karen lived in two upper floors in Bait Ashereef, one floor being her flat and the other floor being where she ran a weaving school for Muslim women. She transferred to less suitable accommodation in the School, so that the Budds could have her flat, with Jack having the middle floor for the club. This was a surprise to everyone, but Karen had great joy in doing it at the Lord's leading. So when Kath and the children arrived on 12th October 1952, there was an adequate flat all ready.

4. Around this time, Dr. Walker also moved, to work in a hospital in Tiberias in Israel. He had been invited to Israel on a courtesy visit, at the Israeli Government's expense, to honour him for all the help he had given to Yemenite Jews. Dr. Herbert Torrence, the Superintendent of the Church of Scotland Mission Hospital in Tiberias, Israel, was retiring. He wrote to Dr. Walker saying, 'You are the man to replace me.' Dr. Walker believed that it was of the Lord and left Aden on 9th February 1953.

3

No Fixed Abode

Jack and Kath Budd opened their home in Aden to us and it became our 'Team' headquarters. Our primary task was evangelism in a difficult and unrewarding field. And part of the preparation was the chore of studying Arabic, a very difficult language.

For some months there was no further leading from the Lord and we found it very frustrating. Yet it was a time when the Lord was preparing the way for establishing an indigenous church in Aden. And we had encouragements seeing the work of the Holy Spirit among RAF personel.

Ron Harbottle was stationed in the RAF Camp at Steamer Point. He came to stay at Jack's flat for a week's leave. Towards the end of the week, he asked if he could have a talk with me. He opened his heart and told me that his Christian life had become very dry and empty. He felt he would just have to go back into the world, and have his fill of what the world had to offer. He said, 'I know where I am, Romans 7, and I know where I want to be, in Romans 8, but how to get there I don't know.'

I spoke to him about salvation and redemption, and why we should accept God's tremendous gift with thanksgiving and praise. If we desire to respond in a way that would really please God and rejoice his Holy Spirit, it should be a complete and unconditional surrender of our lives and bodies, according to the terms of Romans 12:1-2. We could ask the Lord for the gift and fullness of his Holy Spirit (Luke 11:13) to empower us to enter into and complete God's will and purpose for us. 'Yes, yes,' he said, 'I know these things, but how to get there is the problem.'

That Friday afternoon, Ron went for a walk with Lionel along the rocky coast and they spoke together on these things. Ron was still not able to enter into the reality of appropriating them. But that evening he burst into the room where I was, and took my hands in both of his, his face just glowing with joy. 'Oh Bev!' he said, 'I just want to tell you that I have put Luke 11: 13 on the credit side of my account.' Ron had been trained as an accountant, and was working in the accounts department in the RAF.

The RAF Padre had asked him to preach on the Sunday morning. Arriving at the Chapel he was terribly concerned, as he had not been able to get a message together. He went forward, intending to apologize. On the table was a Bible. He glanced down at it and his eye fixed on Luke 11:13. He told those assembled that he had been about to confess that he didn't have a message, but that he now knew what he had to speak about and proceeded to give a powerful address. After the service a number of the believing airmen gathered round him, asking, 'What has happened to you, Ron?' He told them that he had given his life wholly and unconditionally to the Lord Jesus Christ. He said that he had asked the Lord for his Holy Spirit to be Lord of his life and to empower him for his service. Five of them gave their lives fully to the Lord and he worked in a very wonderful way in and through them. Later Ron and some of the others were called by the Lord to join what came to be The Red Sea Mission Team.

The believers had a good deal of freedom to run their meetings, so they started having three prayer meetings a week, two of them before their regular meetings. At one of the meetings they discussed about how to pray effectively. They felt they should all agree to pray for something they could be sure the Lord wanted (1 John 5:14-15). They all agreed they were a small group of believers, surrounded with a great number of unsaved. They felt they should ask for the salvation of as many as they could believe for. They all said they could believe for six souls in the month.

There were six very definite conversions. Tough airmen, who were foul-mouthed and heavy drinkers, were really transformed. They were given moral courage to kneel by their beds to pray, despite the abuse and boots thrown at them. They bought Reference Bibles from the Danish Mission Bible shop and joined the believers in the meetings. The Lord was drawing them on in faith, and honouring the faith they were exercising in him.

For the next month, July, the boys felt that they should ask the Lord for three souls by name. Remarkably, the three named were converted during the month. Each one testified how the Lord had dealt with him.

Jack and Kath's home was open to these boys to come in groups for meals, and many of them spent week-ends or a week's leave there. Lionel and Jack were used in building them up in faith and in giving them missionary vision. Ron was used of the Lord as their spiritual leader, but the Lord was also using each one of them.

One could see a pattern of the Lord leading them on in faith. As I mentioned, in June they prayed for six to be saved. In July, they prayed for three by name and each was converted, the last one coming through near the end of the month. In August, they prayed for another three by name, but it was not until the last few days of the month that the three were converted. Faith, as it was increasing, was having to be exercised, and was tested more. In September and October there were no apparent answers to the definite prayer requests they made. What lessons we all have to learn. Is it that the Spirit is grieved? Is it that faith is being further exercised and tested? The children of Israel had to learn to trust, not only when they saw wonders, but also when God seemed to leave them.

I was still welcome to do evangelistic work in the Keith Falconer Hospital at Sheikh Othman. This was an excellent opportunity for the gospel. Arabic recordings were a great help. When starting in a ward, I would often feel the tension and opposition. Nevertheless, some would listen and accept Gospels and other portions of Scripture. When a Muslim had already read a portion, we found he was much more ready to have another portion, and much more open to hear what we had to say, even if previously he had seemed very closed. In the wards, if new patients objected, the others would tell them to be quiet and listen; later they too would be more receptive. To see the Word of God received by Muslims was a deeply satisfying experience. Yet it was but seed sowing. We knew that if some came to believe, for them to actually come out of Islam and stand for the Lord Jesus would be a tremendous thing. The power of Satan in Islam is really crushing against any such new found faith.

Once, a patient I had not particularly noticed before beckoned me over to his bed, his face shining. He had a Gospel of Matthew in his hand and was pointing to 8:26: 'Then he arose, and rebuked the winds and the sea; and there was a great calm.' He said to me, 'He has done that in my heart.' I asked the doctor about him and discovered he was a shopkeeper. One day he had fled from his shop into the mountains, berserk, as if a thousand demons were after him. He was found after a week, in a terrible state of physical and nervous exhaustion, and brought to the hospital. The doctor was quite amazed at the change in the man and the fact that he had been remarkably delivered. To me, the Lord had done a far greater miracle in his heart than stilling the storm on the lake. The man was brought up as a Muslim, yet he knew that it was the Lord Jesus who had delivered him. The Word of God had become alive to him.

Once a week we would go out selling Gospels, other Scripture portions, Bibles and New Testaments, mostly in Arabic, but also in Urdu and some of the Indian languages. I always found this a great strain, partly because I hate trying to sell anything and am very poor at it, but also because there was very real and fierce Satanic opposition. We would go into shops or speak to people in the streets or markets. Aden seemed to be almost exclusively a city of men. The very few women one saw were covered from head to foot in black Shaydahs, apart from a silk veil just over their eyes. The rest were confined to their houses, peering through heavily latticed windows, or enjoying only the cloudless sky from their small courtyards.

On one occasion a large crowd had gathered around me in a market square. One man pushed his way to just in front of me and said in a very threatening way, 'Who is Jesus Christ?' The others took up the cry, 'Yes! Answer! Who is Jesus Christ?' My first reaction was to risk a very great aggravation of an already nasty situation by declaring the truth unequivocally. It was on my lips to say that Jesus Christ is the Son of the Living God. But I was in touch with the throne of grace and asking for strength and grace to continue. The Lord gave me insight to see that the question was not sincere, but intended to create the maximum trouble. He also, at the same moment, put into my mind the answer that I was to give, an answer I had never thought of using before.

I raised my hands, gesturing for quiet, and the murmuring died down. They were ready to listen. I think most of them thought they would hear words that would inflame the crowd, and were looking forward to seeing the expected consequences. I told them that if a great Sultan goes far away for a long time, many of his subjects may think they can say what they like about him. Also, they think they can do things against his interests and against his servants without fear, as he is not there to see what they are doing. However, if there is word that he is returning, they begin to fear what will happen when he finds out what they have said and done. (I knew that the Koran speaks about the Second Coming of Jesus, but to the Muslims, it is to hand over the Kingdom to Mohammed.) I continued, 'Jesus, the Messiah, is coming again soon. He will hold you responsible for what you have said about him, and for what you have done to his servants.'

One and another among the crowd began saying, 'Yes! He is coming soon. He is coming soon.' Just then a picture came into my mind of the Lord passing through the midst of a hostile crowd and departing. I turned and walked through the crowd, and as I left them I heard a swelling tumult of voices, many saying, 'That is right. He is coming again.' Words of Scripture became very meaningful to me, 'When thou goest through the waters I will be with thee, and the floods shall not overflow thee.'

We found that John's Gospel was the best for Muslim work. It starts, 'In the beginning was the Word.' The Koran only depicts Jesus as a great and special Prophet, not divine, yet it calls him, 'Kalimet Allah' (The Word of God). This they accept, and by the time they get to John 3:16, which clearly shows that we are saved by the Son of God, the Word has gripped their hearts and they want to know more. One who has read John's Gospel is usually very ready to take other books. Luke's Gospel is also good, even for a start. Matthew's Gospel, starting with a long genealogy, tends to cause them to lose interest before they get far enough into it. I have heard that Matthew is best for the Chinese, as they have ancestor worship. To them, anyone with such a genealogy as the Lord

Jesus must have been a very great person indeed.

Mark's Gospel starts with, 'The beginning of the gospel of Jesus Christ, the Son of God.' This immediately arouses the fierce opposition of Muslims. The Bible Society issued Mark in Arabic with a tough linen cover, making it very difficult to tear up. I would not advise using Mark with Muslims unless the Lord clearly led to do so. I add this qualification though. I met an young Arab in Aden and it was clear that he was trusting the Lord Jesus as his Saviour. I asked him how he had come to know the Lord and he told me that a few years before Dr. Gurney had given him a Mark's Gospel.

In the evenings, I was very often helping Jack in the Boys Club. During the day we had frequent visits from Arabs, Somalis and others who had been contacted through colportage, the Club or other ways. It was uphill work; some would come for a while and we would not see them again. Others would continue and we would see the Word of God gripping their hearts.

One such was a fisherman who became deeply interested. He came to the point of wanting to repent of his sins and to ask the Lord Jesus to forgive him and save him. He asked if he could come to church with us that night, Sunday 6th June 1953. Some Arabs must have seen him going into the Church of Scotland building for when we came out there was a crowd with stones waiting for him. Dr. Raymond Smith took him out the back way to his car and drove him to a bus stop. It was two months after this before we saw him again, but his faith seemed real, it had withstood the blast of fear. Even a year and a half later, on the occasions that we saw him, he seemed to be bright and have a real love for the Lord. However, such is the heartbreak of work in Islam, one day we found him with others chewing qart[1]. After this we could see that his joy had gone and he drifted away from the Lord. The Lord warns, 'Watch and pray that ye enter not into temptation.'

Another young man contacted through the Club was a nineteen-year-old Somali from Hargeisa, who was on holiday in Aden. As I knew more Arabic, Jack handed him over to me. I found him to be a sincere seeking soul. Lionel gave him an Arabic New Testament. Two days later, he seemed to have real assurance of salvation and was really grateful to us for leading him to Christ. He was hungry for the Word and responded to the exhortation to full and unconditional surrender to the Lord to do his will. He spent whatever time he could with us until he had to return to Somaliland, which was closed to the gospel. Later, we heard that three other Somalis had been converted through his witness and the four of them

---

1. This is the name of a plant, grown mostly in Ethiopia, where it is called chetty. Its leaves contain a powerful ephedrine type drug. It is a real scourge in South Arabia and to some extent in Ethiopia. A bunch of the sprigs sells for the equivalent of a day's wages for a labourer. When they start chewing the leaves, it grips them in addiction. It makes them wide awake, yet languid, when they should be getting sleep, and stirs their sexual desires and imaginations. It is the ruination of many lives and families. There are queues waiting to buy up the stuff when a plane load arrives several times a week. The buyers make big profits retailing it to the victims of its addiction.

were meeting for Bible study and prayer, twice a week. It was a cause for great praise that there was a tiny indigenous church growing in that fast-closed land.

Despite being involved in Muslim work, the deep conviction of my ultimate call to the Jews never left me. I kept up with the study of Hebrew. Many times when Lionel saw the Hebrew grammar book coming out, I was sure he thought that I had it in mind to leave him, and that he had failed to 'hook' me for Muslim work.

4

Aden Missions and their Fruit

There was a very good relationship between the various missions in Aden. I am sure that the weekly inter-mission prayer meeting, every Friday afternoon, had a good deal to do with this. It was held in turn at each mission. News and requests were shared for praise and prayer. It was also a happy time of fellowship. Two missions in particular deserve to be mentioned in more detail: the Church of Scotland Mission and the Danish Mission.

The Church of Scotland Mission was the longest-standing Protestant Mission in Aden. It began on 8th December 1886 with the arrival of the Hon. Ian Keith Falconer. They had the Keith Falconer Mission Hospital at Sheikh Othman, a town of about 30,000. At the best they had three doctors, two running the hospital of eighty beds, and one seconded to the Government as Protectorate Medical Officer. There were two qualified Sisters, with a locally trained, unqualified staff.

Dr. Ahmed Affara had been a teacher at the Mission School. He came to faith in Christ and asked for baptism, stressing it had to be done publicly. The resultant furore was so strong that Dr. Petrie had to send him out of the country to save his life. His father built a mosque to atone for his son's sin. After qualifying as a doctor he returned to serve in the same hospital. He was received coldly at first by the

Muslims, but later won their hearts by his love and skill. Patients came from all over Yemen to 'Affara's' Hospital. He married Nasra, who was Marouf's sister. Later, though a believing Christian, he was elected Mayor of Muslim Sheikh Othman.

Through their work in the Protectorate, Hassan Ali, one of the Protectorate medical dressers of the Subeihi Tribe, had accepted Christ, and stood his ground well. He had a little group, of those who were interested, for Bible study.

The local staff at the hospital were quite loyal, but solidly Muslim. However, one of the dressers, Mohammed Ali, made a profession of faith and was baptized along with his wife Aisha and their two little girls. Later, I heard that he had been hospitalized with TB and put on half (his meagre) pay.

I wondered how I could help his weak faith, if indeed he had any. I went to him and saw he was reading an Arabic Bible and his face was shining. He told me that he was reading about the Passover Lamb being sacrificed, and the blood applied to the door frame. Israel was then able to escape from slavery to Pharaoh. He said to me that that was what the Lord Jesus had done for us in dying on the Cross. I had been wondering how I could console him, and he had given me a tremendous heart lift. I saw that the Holy Spirit was feeding him from God's Word.

Later, Aisha was also hospitalized with amoebic abscess of the liver. She used to see and hear me, through a lattice, taking gospel recordings in the men's wards. She called to me, 'Brother Bev! The women need this as well.' I said I couldn't, but she asked Dr.

Smith to give me permission, and he agreed for me to try.

When I had played gospel recordings to the women, and spoken in my poor Arabic, Aisha would then, out of a full heart, retell them in a way that was fully understandable to the ladies. She would then take Scriptures, give some to each woman, saying that those at home who could read should read to them. One day when I had spoken on the Prodigal Son, I could see that most of the women were interested. So, when Aisha retold it, pouring out her heart to them and telling how it was just like the love of God for us, waiting and yearning for us to repent and come back to him, many of the women were sobbing, tears pouring down their cheeks. Islam has nothing like it. Allah is depicted as very remote, unapproachable, arbitrary and very capricious, with not a breath of love.

Of course, it didn't mean that they were angels. On one occasion, Aisha had a quarrel with another woman in the hospital compound. They were scratching each other and pulling each other's hair out. Suddenly, Aisha saw a bottle, flew for it, and seizing it by the neck, shattered the other end against a rock. She was going to jab it into the other woman's face, but bystanders were able to drag the two apart.

The next day, Aisha went broken with remorse to Mrs. Affara, wondering how the Lord could forgive her, and how the Christians could forgive her for so disgracing the Lord. This was a miracle of his grace, as in the natural sense they never confess nor ask for forgiveness, but only present excuses.

Mustafa was another of those precious trophies of

grace, and worked in the Protectorate under Dr. Walker. Mustafa was witnessing and giving Bible portions to many. Quardhy Mansoor was very angry at this. When Mustafa asked the Quardhy, he admitted that he had not read the Bible. Mustafa told him it was a very good book and it was not right for a judge to condemn it, not having read it. The Quardhy accepted a Bible from Mustafa. Rather than finding out what was wrong with it, it gripped his heart. As I have written in Chapter 2, when I met the Quardhy some time later, he had read the Bible six times. His wife once asked Dr. Gurney, 'Do you believe the miracles?' He said, 'I do!' She replied, 'So do I!'

Mustafa was married to Shofeeqah in 1951. It was an event of very great joy. Two of the precious trophies, won at such great cost, joined in marriage to form, so far as is known, the first believing Christian family in Aden from a Muslim background.

The Danish Mission in Aden
Oluf Hojer of Denmark was burdened to take the gospel to Arabia and a small committee was formed to support him. The Danish work was commenced in Aden with the signing of a cooperation agreement with the Church of Scotland Mission on 26th July 1904. On 1st July 1946 the Danish work was absorbed into the Danish Missionary Society, the foreign missionary arm of the evangelical wing of the Danish State Lutheran Church.

In Aden in 1953 they had several staff, some of whom had been there for over twenty-five years. The mission ran a school with about 120 Muslim girls, with a number of Muslim lady teachers on the staff. They also had a hand weaving and handicraft school,[1] mainly for teaching divorced Muslim women a means of earning a livelihood. These women were often in a dreadful plight. If a man was displeased with one of his wives, he only had to say, 'I divorce you,' and the marriage was annulled, unless he changed his mind. Under Muslim law, if he said, 'I divorce you!' three times, they could not be remarried. The divorced wife was at the mercy of relatives to support her. Sometimes she was allowed to take her child or children. These women had no training to earn a living and there were almost no openings for them for employment.

The Danish Mission also took responsibility for opening a Mission Station in Mudia, about 3,000 ft. up in the mountains of the Protectorate, about 170 miles from Aden.

Some of their fruit

Mubarak (Blessed) had come to faith through the Danish Mission. He had taken his stand and been baptized in 1923, and was to be found regularly in the services, including communion. He looked after the Danish Mission Bible Shop in Aden Crater. He was to some extent in the grip of 'Qart,' and the vital glow of his witness was somewhat dimmed by the pressure. He was able to show his mettle again before he died.

---

1. In the centre of the crowded market stood 'Bait Ashereef,' the Danish Church occupying the ground floor. As we have seen (page 23), the middle floor had been used for the weaving school, and the top floor as Karen's flat, but these were given over for use to the Budds.

There was also Nuri, who was the widow of one who had indeed stood for Christ. She was a simple lady and I think she believed. She was helped by the Mission and was always glad to see the Danish Mission ladies, but there was no fire, no witness.

Shofeeqah was different. She had been through the Danish Mission School but had been taken away early by her family to be married. The husband later divorced her and the family had her married again. This husband also divorced her. From one of the marriages she had a boy, Emil. Somewhere along the line Shofeeqah came through to faith and took a clear stand. She was indeed a miracle of grace. As mentioned on page 37, she married Mustafa.

After a few years of very bright witness, there were whisperings, rumours and accusations against Mustafa. This was not at all an uncommon thing against converts; but many times it was just scurrilous and malicious slander. As in other cases the missionaries just brushed these rumours aside. Then it was found that some of the serious accusations were true. More things were looked into, and even more dreadful things were confirmed as fact. The missionaries were very angry, largely I think because Mustafa had managed to bluff them.

There was a meeting of senior missionaries with Mustafa and Shofeeqah. On that same day all the ground was cut from under them. They were put out of the church, Mustafa was dismissed from his job, and they had to vacate the house they were living in, which belonged to the hospital. They were indeed in dire straights. Some felt at the time that this was a very serious over-reaction. It requires great wisdom and patience to find the mind of the Lord on such occasions when feelings and emotions are running high. With time for prayer and serious thought, the dreadful consequences would not have been difficult to predict.

Mustafa accepted the enemy's way of escape to go back to Islam. The whole work suffered a stunning blow. It seemed to have been a well coordinated, devilish plan.

Sometime later, I met Mustafa and had a talk with him. He was terribly bitter against the missionaries. There seemed no sign of repentance on his part. However, what he told me was very illuminating. A short while before the showdown, some very wealthy Arabs, whom he had never met before, were coming to him offering him jobs with staggering salaries and a big house if he would leave the Mission. One of these men took him to a big, beautifully furnished house in Aden Crater and said that it was his if he would accept the above terms. Mustafa said to me that he could not understand it, nor what was behind it. He told me that when the showdown came, he just had no other choice but to go back to Islam. Being put out of the Church of Scotland Mission, no other Mission would have him; if he remained a Christian, no one else would have him. Of course he could have sought the Lord and come back to him in repentance, but he was too full of blaming everyone else but himself. He had torn up their Bibles and hymn books.

When the Body of Christ is joined in love, in something of the unity in Spirit that transcends national and denominational barriers, there is a deep sense of pain when one or another suffers. It is difficult to convey the pain that was felt corporately by the Lord's people in Aden and elsewhere when, on Friday 18th September 1953, the news went round that Mustafa and Shofeeqah had gone back to Islam. It was, on the contrary, a cause of great jubilation in Islam, and no doubt in hell. The news was broadcast from all the mosques in Aden, and throughout Yemen.

Later Mustafa had an interview with the King of the Yemen, and was invited to practice medicine there, which he accepted. Subsequently, he divorced Shofeeqah and married another couple of wives. Shofeeqah was forced by her family to remarry again. What a tangle, what a mess. Maybe, if the missionaries had disciplined him, reduced his pay, but given him a chance, who knows?

Over the next few years I met him occasionally. Once, he asked for a Bible and a hymn book and said that he had tried to come back to the Lord, but could not. We spoke with him and prayed, but there seemed an awful hardness. Soon after the break, Shofeeqah said that whatever happened she wanted to go on with the Lord Jesus. Many people over the years never ceased to bear them up before the Lord.

To understand a little of what this meant takes one into the heart of something of the joys as well as the travail and heartbreak of taking the gospel to the Muslims. It would be a gross understatement to say that there are easier fields than Islam, yet Christ's commission is 'to every creature', and on some he lays the call to Islam. When one considers all the love and sacrifice over the years of mission, since the work was opened in Aden by Keith Falconer, it is a source of wonder to see how so many have left the comforts and security of home and loved ones to go to such an unpromising field. The language is a terrible barrier to overcome before one can even start to get to grips with the task. Then there is the overpowering heat of a seven months' summer, the sweat, prickly heat, flies, smells and tropical diseases, as well as the usual ills. Very few ever really master the language, they are usually swamped trying to meet so many needs of those they have come out to minister to.

Then there is the fierce opposition of Islam to the gospel. Lionel used a very apt illustration to show the hold Islam has. In photography, when a film is put in the developing solution, it can be made lighter or darker, but once it has been in the fixing solution the developer has no effect on it. When the gospel reaches pagan tribes held in darkness by animism, spirit worship, idols and witch doctors, there can often be spectacular results. Even in a short time, whole tribes can turn to Christ. However, if Islam reaches a tribe before the gospel, it is 'fixed'. Missionaries can work there for many years and hardly see any results. In Islam, Satan has a superb system of keeping souls in darkness.

5

The Red Sea Mission Team Founded

About the beginning of July 1953, Lionel received a letter from Miss Elsa Gundersen, saying that the Lord had laid it upon her to come out and join us. She believed that it was to look after a headquarters. This was rather remarkable as Elsa was fifty-six at the time, and her call was to come out to a pioneering area, which was not exactly a health resort, even for a much younger person. She was a qualified teacher. Her life had the fragrance of Mary's alabaster box of spikenard, just broken, and poured out in love for her Lord.

Elsa was one of those who had responded to a request by Emperor Haile Selassie to Dr. Bob Thompson of the SIM Mission in Ethiopia to recruit fifty Christian teachers from the USA and Canada for Ethiopia. She worked in Ethiopia for some years, but had to return to Canada because of a skin condition that would not clear up. She had an eighty-acre farm on very fertile land in Alberta, Canada, I think at Red Deer. She worked the farm so that the proceeds could go to Dr. Gurney for the work in the Red Sea area, she having come to know him in Ethiopia and caught the vision of the needs. The Lord then called her to teach at the Prairie Bible Institute in Three Hills, Alberta. She arranged for her farm to be run by a small committee of Christian farmers, with the proceeds going to the Red Sea work.

The idea of a headquarters appealed to Lionel as we had no HQ of our own. Jack, too, was very keen on the idea. Lionel really did try to get a headquarters. First he had the idea of an Inter-mission Rest House in Dhalla, 5,000 feet up in the mountains of the Protectorate. He thought that it could also serve as our Team HQ, with Elsa to look after it. There was a good response from the Missions, but eventually nothing came of it. There were another five promising possibilities but the door definitely closed on each one.

Lionel wrote to Elsa, 'Dear Elsa, are you sure that this leading you had is really from the Lord? Personally, I very much doubt it. I have really tried to get a headquarters for you to run, but every door has closed.'

The reply came from Elsa, 'Please don't try to get a headquarters for me to run. The Lord is going to do that.'

This really was of the Lord, as later events showed, and he had given Elsa the full assurance of faith to declare it. Looking back, we could clearly see how the Lord closed doors that were not of him, but many times opened doors that were of him, in very wonderful ways. 'He openeth and no man shutteth, he shutteth and no man openeth.'

Dr. Allan Fawdry, the Port Health Officer, was a dedicated Christian and a good friend of Lionel. Through him we were able to have a free trip up the Red Sea, including calls at Djibouti, Massawa and Assab.

Apart from the captain, the Italian engineer and one Hadhramaut Arab, the nine remaining members of the crew were all Danakil, the first I had ever seen. They were all very friendly, one of them particularly, as he wanted to learn English. His name was Mukhaddin, literally, 'the brains of the religion'. He wanted me to teach him the alphabet and words. Throughout the trip we had a good deal of time together and it was a good opening for the gospel. He also taught me some of the Danakil language, Afar.

We regarded this trip as helping confirm our call to work with the Danakil. The trip had not been of our arranging. The boat had a predominantly Danakil crew. We had been taken to the southern border of Dankalia, to Djibouti; then we were taken to the northern limit of Danakil territory, to Massawa; then also to Assab which is in Danakil territory.

On 17th August 1953, a few days after we returned from our trip, we had a Team Field Conference. Unfortunately Marion was in Mudia. When we gave an account of the trip, there was very lively discussion. We had a unanimous conviction that the Lord was calling us to open up work in this fanatically Muslim Bedouin Tribe, the Danakil. (They do not like the name and call themselves 'the Afar'; their language, which was then unwritten, is also known as Afar.)

It was resolved that we should attempt an opening in Massawa, possibly in October. However, we were to see later that place, time and means were all in the mighty, capable hands of our faithful, sovereign Lord Jesus. This would not be according to our planning and arranging, but according to his gracious leading and enabling.

Directly after our conference, Lionel wrote a circular letter telling something of our trip, and of how the Lord was making plain that he wanted us to open work in Dankalia.

About a month later Lionel received a letter from David Stokes, Field Leader of the BCMS work in Ethiopia. He said, as Lionel knew well, that Danakil was very much on their hearts because it was a Field allocated to BCMS by the Emperor. Since Lionel had gone they had never had an opportunity nor the personnel to make an entry. David was indeed very happy to hear of the way the Lord was leading us to establish a work there, but informed us that according to Ethiopian regulations, each mission *had* to have a headquarters in Addis Ababa. He then said, 'Why not share a headquarters with us? And by the way, do you have anyone to run it?'

When Lionel told David of Elsa Gundersen's leading, David, who knew Elsa well from her time in Ethiopia, replied, 'Dear Elsa, the very one!'

Lionel was deeply grateful to the Lord, for he was able to write to Elsa that the Lord had very clearly confirmed to us her call, and the very thrilling news about the headquarters, and how the Lord was honouring her faith.

By 1953 we had five members of our Team in Aden, and our honorary Secretary, Gypsie Perkins, in Britain. Our Home Office was Gypsie's small bed-sitting room in a retirement home in Parkstone, Dorset. It is worth saying something concerning how each of the five were involved at this stage of the Team's development.

52

1953 had been a really frustrating time for Lionel. We had no work of our own; the small nucleus of the Team on the field was indeed a mere grain of mustard seed, with three out of the five seconded to the Danish Mission; and we had no field headquarters of our own.

Lionel was able to catch up on his correspondence, and be in touch with prospective candidates, as well as with praying people who had the burden of Islam and the Red Sea work on their hearts. He did have a few trips, taking various people up into the Protectorate, as he could drive a Landrover, and knew the tracks, as well as the language and the people. Such trips were always a release for him.

He spent time making contact with Muslims in the streets and inviting some home for deeper talks. A group of five Yemenites that he had contacted came each day for a talk. On one occasion he went to get cold drinks for them and later found that his alarm watch was missing. After a week or two he met them and asked about the watch, but they denied all knowledge of it. However, he told them that it must not make any difference and they were still welcome. They did come again on occasions.[1]

It was Lionel's faith that inspired faith in us all. If any joined the Team under the impression that Lionel had the resources, they would soon find out that he hadn't. They would have to start trusting the Lord for themselves. Nevertheless, the care of all the Team members was his constant prayer burden before the Lord.

1. This contact has a bearing on the birth of an indigenous church in Aden after sixty-seven years of missionary work. One of these Yemenites, Yahya, will be heard of later in this context.

While Lionel and myself were absolutely one in our love for the Lord and in our desire to serve him and extend his kingdom, there were times when we had our differences over interpretation of Scripture. Sometimes we would get into really heated arguments. Lionel would make a point and I would say, 'Oh no, brother,' and opening my Bible would say, 'Look at this verse.' Lionel would then give me a verse and it would go on and on, getting more and more heated. Then, sometimes one, sometimes the other, would stop and say, 'Dear brother, this is not in the Spirit,' and the other would realize it too. His arm would go round my shoulder, 'Let us get down before the Lord.' Then we would tell the Lord that we were sorry, often with tears, and ask him to give us light on these points of difference. We would embrace, 'Dear old Bev,' 'Dear old Li.' Unity in the Spirit would be restored.

Jack and Kath Budd were the backbone of the Team, partly because they were the only family and their home was the Team field headquarters. But they also had very special qualities. They both had a keen sense of responsibility and exhibited such faithfulness and loyalty that one could completely rely on them and never be let down. Jack had a remarkable gift for organization. If he had to arrange meetings or events, whether small and simple, or big and complicated, he did not have to sit down and make plans and lists. Somehow he saw the whole picture in his mind and how the various parts different ones had to play fitted together. He just asked different ones to do such and such and when, and so long as they did their parts the whole thing would go like clockwork. He was also careful to check that each understood their part, and how it fitted in with others, and also reminded people in good time as needed.[2]

It is not surprising that at one of our very early Field Council meetings, on 2nd October 1953, Jack was appointed Field Secretary. It was surely the Lord's arranging, as he was still continuing in this key post twenty years later, with the Team having grown to about forty missionaries on the field. His special qualities, complementing those of Lionel, were just the ones needed for building up the Team.

The Boys Club went very well, despite the times of organized opposition, and was an excellent way of establishing long-term contacts with Arab and Somali youths.

Jack's heart and soul was in colportage. In the natural sense this is far from what anyone would chose, particularly to Muslims. At the end of February 1953, Mr. Ashley, the Regional Agent for the British and Foreign Bible Society, who had his headquarters in Addis Ababa, visited Aden. After discussions with Mission leaders, he proposed that Jack be appointed Sub-Agent for part of the region. This appointment was not ratified until 1957, but meanwhile Jack worked very closely with Mr. Ashley.

In all these things Kath was a true helpmeet, working away at the language, and bringing up two young, high-spirited boys. Their home continued to

2. Jack had been active in arranging big interdenominational evangelistic campaigns. He also had a good deal of experience in youth work, having been actively involved in the Young Life Campaign.

be a highway for the Lord, with so many coming for meals, and often staying with them. All this despite the heat, dust, flies and having to look to the Lord for every penny. For the first four and a half years we had no salary; each was looking to the Lord, but the Lord was wonderfully faithful. For myself there were times when I lived using about three shillings a day for some weeks, and then there would be a remarkable deliverance. The last year I was with the Team we had an allowance of £10 each per month. It was continually a living testimony to the truth of his promise, 'Seek ye first the kingdom of God and his righteousness, and all these things shall be added unto you.'

Since her arrival in October 1952 Marion Thomas had been able to stay at the hospital in Sheikh Othman. She was concentrating on Arabic study but was able to help in the hospital, for which they were grateful. Acclimatization, growing to know and love the people, and getting tropical medicine experience, were invaluable to her.

In March 1953, the Danish Mission asked for Marion to help in their station in Mudia. This was a very good opening for her, and there was an agreement that could be terminated with three months notice either side. Marion went to Mudia on 6th April. Her companion was the veteran Danish missionary, Miss Mette Skovhus, a teacher who really loved and understood the Arabs, and they loved her. Marion did very well there and was much loved.

The name 'Red Sea Mission Team' was first agreed upon at the Council meeting that appointed Jack as Field Secretary. Present at that meeting were Lionel, Jack, Kath, Marion and myself, the sum total of the Team on the field at that time.

I stated that I knew someday I would have to go to Israel, as this was something that the Lord had shown me, and was the condition I had made on joining Dr. Gurney. However, I requested that, if and when the Lord opened the door for me to go to Israel, I might remain a member of the Red Sea Mission Team. There was silence for a while, then Lionel said that he had thought and prayed about this possibility. He had realized that although we would still be one in Spirit, it would have to be goodbye to the Team if I went to Israel. He said, 'If there were links, Bev, we would be suspect by the Arabs because of you, and you may be suspect in Israel because of your links with us. I see no way.' I recognized that this was God's wisdom, God's way. The point was registered in the minutes of that meeting.

The first printed News Letter, No.1, was published March 1955, headed 'THE RED SEA MISSION TEAM is an Interdenominational, International, Evangelical Team of consecrated men and women, called of God, dedicated to reaching those fast bound in Islam. It is not a new competing Mission, but a Team, cooperating with existing evangelical agencies, sincerely desiring to work with all Bible-honouring, Christ-loving groups engaged in the evangelization of Muslims, and welcoming their fellowship. Their objective is that the Lord Jesus may be made known soon to Muslims everywhere, and especially to unreached tribes around the Red Sea (John 17:21, Nehemiah 4:19-20, Rev. 7:9-10).'

As the Team grew, we became a motley crew: such different types, different denominational backgrounds, different nationalities. The calling of the Lord to each one was so clear that they and we knew it was of him. This was our unity despite our different backgrounds.

6

Onward – to Danakil

Lionel had arranged with David Stokes that he should go to Addis Ababa to see about a site for the headquarters as well as the possibilities for the Danakil work. It was agreed that, all being well, I should join Lionel in Addis some time later. Lionel flew to Djibouti on the 9th of October. While there, he contacted Mohammed Masri who had accepted Christ during our time in Abyan. He had moved to Djibouti because of the pressure and persecution of Christians in Aden by Moslems. He was still rather fearful. It is easy for us to judge, but who knows how many of the people of western democracies would hold on to the name of Christ in such crushing circumstances.

Since Lionel went to Addis by plane, he had had to travel light, so I undertook to take all our luggage to Addis. The Lord provided the perfect solution; how safe to trust him and to walk with him. Allan Fawdry heard of the problem and told me that A. Besse & Co. had many big petrol lorries travelling daily from Assab to Addis Ababa. He took me to see Tony Besse who asked about our work and the journey. He then kindly arranged for me to make the three day journey with all the luggage without charge. He also gave me a signed letter instructing Besse's employees and agents to give me all the help I needed. The luggage amounted to twenty heavy boxes and tin trunks with medical, household and personal goods. With my visible resources it seemed impossible to get it all to Addis Ababa, but in the end all I had to pay for was a truck to take the boxes to Aden harbour, and a one-way deck passage on one of Besse's Dhows.

Eritrea - Danakil

We arrived at Assab at on Monday evening, but anchored outside, and tied up at early the next morning. The crew put the cases ashore and I gave Tony Besse's letter to his representative who arranged for his men to take the cases through Customs, and then for them to be put in Besse's store for the night, except for a few personal things I needed. The cases were to be loaded on the petrol tanker the next morning. The Customs Officer was very thorough, but in examining the scriptures, he asked if he could have a French New Testament, which I was very pleased to give to him. He let everything go through without charge. I then went to the SIM house, where George and Doreen Leighton kindly invited me to stay with them and we had very good fellowship.

George took me to meet the District Officer who was the Administrator of Southern Danakil. Sheikh Musa Ga'as[1] was a Danakil and spoke English fairly well. George had already told him that Lionel was hoping to open dispensaries in Danakil, and Sheikh Musa had seemed to be pleased at the prospect. Indeed he was most friendly.[2]

---

1. He was to be one of the key figures the Lord used to grant us the openings into the Danakil tribe.

2. Later, I understood the desperate medical need. There was one doctor in Assab, who also ran a small hospital, not really

60

On Wednesday morning, the twenty-ton petrol tanker and trailer arrived with all the boxes roped on. The burly Italian driver was very friendly but could not speak a word of English. I could manage a dozen or so words of Italian, but we got on quite well together, mostly by sign language.

We set off across the barren wilderness of volcanic stones, arriving by noon at Amana, the first Danakil roadside town and composed of tin shacks. The Danakil men were quite well covered, draped with white cloth. Many held a long stick across their shoulders. When they are crossing the desert, they have a small leather pouch of water hanging from one end of the stick and a pouch of grain hanging from the other end. Occasionally they eat a little of the grain and have a sip of the water. They are very dark skinned and are small and wiry. They are a cousin tribe to the Somalis.

I was surprised to notice that the women had only a long cloth skirt, from the waist to the ankles, and nothing else. Married women, however, wear a dark cloth headdress. This was in marked contrast to most Muslim women who are almost, or completely, covered from head to foot. We had lunch at an eating house, then stayed the night at another village. In the

---

enough for Assab itself. To the north, the nearest medical help was another small hospital, having three doctors, in Massawa, 350 miles away. We found that there was one medical dresser, who had had about three months medical training, at Thio, about half way to Massawa. He had a cupboard full of syringes and antibiotics. Each time he gave an injection, the patient developed a deep seated abscess, so he was reduced to using about six ointments only.

cabin of the tanker there were two bunks.

Next morning we set off at 3.20 and by 6 am had started climbing the foothills, where there was some vegetation, which increased the higher we went. We passed very close to a pack of about thirty baboons, some with their young clinging to their mother's backs or necks. It was refreshing to see the first running water since setting off, and there were trees, some with fruit on. We saw a large group of ostriches, and a large vulture, flying very low and slowly, before us, its wings seeming to span the road. There were also quite a number of beautifully coloured birds.

We had breakfast at Sardo, where they had thatched huts, the first I had seen. About 10 am we passed Bartie, the last Danakil village of any size. At noon we were coming to very fertile plains, and about twenty miles away, up in the hills, we could see Dessaye, which is on the highway from Addis to Asmara. We were now coming to a thickly populated area by African standards. It was 8 pm before we had dinner, then after eighteen hours driving we stopped at 10 pm for the night.

On Friday morning, we set off at 4.20, climbing to the edge of the escarpment of the mountains of Ethiopia, and then through the Mussolini tunnel at 10,500ft. The descent was really hair-raising; although the road was good, it was just wide enough for two such lorries to pass. The left-hand side rose at a steep angle and the right side of the road fell away precipitately – and we were driving on the right! The driver must have been extremely tired; it was a tremendous effort for him to keep awake on this third day of marathon driving. He was singing aloud and slapping his face, then his voice would die away, his head would drop and his eyes close, completely oblivious of the terrible danger. Then he would waken with a jolt, size up the situation, and start again singing aloud and slapping his face. This went on for about an hour, and was especially harassing when we descended into cloud and could not see more than fifteen to twenty yards. At times, when I could see that we were easing over towards the edge, I would be just about to seize the wheel, when he would again wake with a start.

I was greatly relieved when we reached the flatter plateau ground. At 9 am, we stopped for breakfast at a wayside eating shack. The cab was warm, but outside, at that altitude of 8,000 ft., it was bitterly cold and I had to put on thicker clothing. The air was very clear and it was possible to see at least a hundred miles. It was a vast area of plateaus, some levels at 3,000 ft., some 8,000, and even 10,000 ft. There must have been every kind of climate, with the possibility of growing every kind of plant and tree at one altitude or another.

Addis Ababa

We arrived at the barrier in Addis at 3.50 pm. I rang up Mr. Ashley of the British and Foreign Bible Society, as Lionel had directed. He asked me to go to Besse's depot and said that he would pick me up there. The driver had insisted on paying for all my meals, and it was only with great difficulty that I got him to accept fifteen Ethiopian dollars, about £2.50. When

Mr. Gutfreund of Besse read Tony Besse's letter he said that he would arrange for all our goods to be taken to the BCMS compound in a pick-up. However, just then Mr. Ashley arrived in a VW Microbus, with the middle seat removed, and he was able to take all the luggage. Lionel must have told him that there would be a lot!

At the Bible Churchman's Missionary Society I received a very warm welcome from Caroline Stokes and Bob and Fern Lucas. Lionel almost ate me. It was great to be with him again, and also to meet Ed Marquart. Ed was a superintendent of schools in Minnesota. The Lord had laid it upon him to represent the Team in the USA, and he had come out to get a first hand view of the fields. That evening I attended my first service in Amharic, and afterwards we had a time of prayer and thanksgiving.

On Saturday, I went with Lionel and Ed into the city to see about visas and other matters, and had my first meal of injura and wut, which is the main meal in Ethiopia. Injura is their bread, like a huge pancake about 1½ to 2 ft. in diameter, looking like tripe and made of partly fermented flour and water. The wut is an exceptionally fiery stew, in a number of varieties including meat wut and lentil wut. The idea is to tear off a piece of injura and to dip it into the wut, then send for the fire brigade, as it is so full of red cayenne pepper.

Lionel pointed out that in the east the thinking is different from the west in so many ways. It is clear that the setting of the Bible is eastern. We think of our main meal as the cooked food, and maybe we have some bread with the main part of the meal. However, here the main meal is the injura, the bread. The wut is just something to help it down. Lionel said that if we should finish the wut before finishing the injura, we could call for more wut, and it would be without charge. If however we finish the injura before the wut, to get more injura we would have to pay for another meal. When the Lord Jesus said, 'I am the Bread of Life,' he meant in the eastern setting, 'I am the *main, basic,* spiritual provision.'

Deliverance of captives

On Sunday morning, I went with Lionel to the big Addis Ababa prison, together with Mr. Bredvej, a Norwegian Christian who was working for Mosvold, a Norwegian shipping and trading firm. We first visited the rigorous punishment and condemned section. Each prisoner had his legs manacled together by heavy iron bands around the ankles, joined with a heavy chain, so that they could only shuffle along. Some had been there for a number of years. The condemned ones may be executed by public hanging fairly quickly, and others after some years. The names of those to be executed each Saturday were submitted to the Emperor on the Friday. When he had signed the order, the names were announced to the prisoners and the ones to be executed would break down into anguished crying and wailing throughout the night. The rest would relax, even if sleep that night was impossible, but the tension would build up again as the week progressed.

It was very moving for me to see the lovely work

of grace that the Lord was doing in this place of tragedy. An elderly prisoner, Tekla Giorgis, when he saw Lionel, shuffled over to some of the other prisoners and brought them over to greet us. It was amazing to see the look of love and joy on their faces, in marked contrast to the other prisoners, even those who had visitors. Tekla was one of those who had come to know the Lord when Lionel had been visiting the prison regularly. Over the years there had been a little group of believers there. Some had been executed, some released, new ones had been led to the Lord by the witness of the believers, and so it had gone on. The talk was all in Amharic, but Mr. Bredvej interpreted for me.

I met a very black young man who was under a death sentence; yet his face was simply radiant. He said that he was so happy that he had come to this place, as it was here, just six months before, he had found Jesus and Jesus had found him. Lionel said to them, 'I suppose that if you should get out of here, you would be taken up with the world again, and forget about these things.' The young man replied to him with John 6:68, 'Lord, to whom shall we go? Thou hast the words of eternal life.' We were answering each other with verses of Scripture. I gave them Luke 4:18, where the Lord Jesus says, 'The Spirit of the Lord is upon me .... to preach deliverance to the captives'; also Hebrews 13:8, 'Jesus Christ the same, yesterday, today, and forever.'

We then went to the other part of the prison to meet Sergeant Guzerheim and three prisoners who had come to know the Lord through him. He also had been led to the Lord by Lionel. It is wonderful how the Lord has his witnesses, even in the most unlikely places. One of the believers had made a wide brimmed straw hat for Lionel, his little love gift.

Amharic studies

In talks with Lionel and Ed, concerning the strategy for tackling Danakil, Lionel felt that I should stay in Addis for three to six months to study Amharic. This would be with the Rev. Cuthbert (Cubby) Dawkins, who taught personnel of all the missions.

The following day, Monday, we went to see Cubby and heard that a new class was starting on the Wednesday which I could join. There were lessons daily in the morning and afternoon. It was a great joy to meet dear Cubby and his wife Thilde. They were so filled with warm Christian love to the Lord and to his children. Cubby had been through Rugby school and Cambridge, and was an ordained Anglican Minister. He had been a colleague of Lionel's in BCMS in his early days in Ethiopia. Thilde was Jewish and had been sent by her family to Britain from Hitler's Germany. Most of her family had perished in the Holocaust. They had six lovely children, and I always felt really welcome in their home, and so often enjoyed rich warm Christian fellowship with them.

On the Wednesday, I started on Amharic with five or six others from the Swedish and Norwegian Missions. The first two weeks were spent in learning the 260 or so letters of the Amharic alphabet.

As for Lionel and Ed, they set off on a trip, across Danakil to Assab, by lorry.

Ma'irgo Buzzabee

On the Sunday afternoon, I attended the Amharic service at BCMS. Sitting next to me in the service was an Ethiopian boy, about sixteen years of age. I spoke to him later and discovered his name was Ma'irgo Buzzabee. I did not know at the time but he was to be a key figure in one of the Lord Jesus's lovely chain reactions. I found that he spoke English well. When I asked him some questions, he said that he was a Coptic Christian, and believed the Bible, and also that Jesus is the Son of God.[3] But he said nobody could know that they were saved and would go to heaven; only God could know. I quoted John 3:16 and said that whoever believes in Jesus has eternal life. He still affirmed that we cannot know. I pointed out his inconsistency: he either did not believe God's Word, or if he believed in Jesus he had eternal life. We went over the same arguments three times. His face suddenly lit up, as he exclaimed, 'Oh! I am saved!' We prayed together and thanked the Lord for the light he had given. The fruit of Christ's mighty victory at Calvary had been registered before my eyes. Ma'irgo came each Sunday, and I found later that he had been a language informant to Cubby Dawkins. It

---

3. At the time I did not know that Coptic Christians accept the authority of the Bible as being higher than the opinions of their religious leaders. This is in contrast to the Roman Catholic Church. The tragedy was that although all the Churches had the Bible, until recent times it had been only in Geez, a dead language, like Latin. Even very few of the priests understood Geez, although they could recite much of it by heart. The Emperor had fought hard to get them to use Amharic Bibles, and by then had managed to do so in about 50% of the Churches.

was evident that the Lord had used me as a link with others in the chain. I gave him some Scriptures on baptism, and also a copy of Dr. Joe Church's, *Every Man A Bible Student*. Later, at the Asfa Wassen School, he gathered about seventeen fellow students for half an hour's daily Bible study.

The Wingate boys

On Sunday, 31st January 1954, I noticed two new faces at the service. Afterwards I found that they were students from the Wingate Secondary School. The name of one was Abainekh Workie, another key figure in the chain reaction. The other was a very quiet boy, Abatay Amdie.

I spoke to Abainekh. He told me that he was a Christian and had eternal life, but I was not convinced. When I asked if he had experienced victory over sin, his head dropped and he could not look me in the eyes. The next Sunday they both came again, and after the meeting Abainekh admitted that he had not experienced salvation in Christ and asked me to help him to understand.

Abatay also wanted the Lord's salvation. He was sincerely ready to repent and to put all his trust in Christ and his atoning death for forgiveness of sins. He was ready also for the living Christ to enter and abide in his heart, to be his Saviour and his Life. I spoke to both of them on victory over sin and Satan by the indwelling of God's Holy Spirit, God's precious Gift to be received by faith by those who receive Christ.

They came on subsequent Sundays, bringing one

or two new students with them. These also were desirous of salvation and each one came to faith in a very real way. Eventually there were eight from Wingate, and one from the Commercial School, as well as Ma'irgo.

Abainekh and some of the others made a full committal of discipleship to the Lord, for his Holy Spirit to fulfil God's purpose for their lives. Abainekh's face was radiant and the Lord was using him as the spiritual leader of the group. They used to walk eight miles each way from the school to the BCMS service. I learned from Abainekh how God had worked. He began searching for God and started going to the American Presbyterian Mission near Wingate. The Ethiopian evangelist realized Abainekh was a hungry soul. Since he also knew Ma'irgo, he advised Abainekh to go to the BCMS and meet Ma'irgo. It was lovely that the evangelist was free from any denominational tug of war spirit, but had the spiritual welfare of Abainekh on his heart.

On the 2nd March, Ma'irgo told me he was fully and unconditionally giving his body to the Lord Jesus for his purposes in the terms of Romans 12:1-2.

Masfin
Masfin's father was one of the chief priests in Addis Ababa. He was active in the Coptic Church, but had been really impressed by the work of grace that the Lord was doing in the hearts of the boys. They brought him to the BCMS service. Masfin came to me and asked many questions. I sought the Lord's wisdom regarding how to answer him. Although he was

convinced that what I said was true, he wanted confirmation from David Stokes, for whom he had a very high regard. He had that talk with David and took the step of faith through the Door, which is Christ, into the Kingdom of God.

Masfin had been given the responsibility for producing the Easter Passion Play for the students, staff and parents at Wingate School. He was converted six days before it was due to be presented. In the days following his conversion, he felt that he should alter a number of parts of the play. He introduced John 3:16, Isaiah 53 and a number of other telling passages. I heard that it had a profound effect, compared with the usual sterile, traditional presentation.

Start of a believers fellowship at Wingate School
I challenged the boys about full surrender and suggested that they gather together for prayer and Bible study twice a week. I was very happy to hear later that they had started meeting as suggested. At first they were meeting outside in a field, but later they had permission to meet in a room at the school.

One day, I arranged to take them all to a service in the Ethiopian Evangelical Church, to introduce them to the fellowship there. Originally this had been the Swedish Mission Church, but when a good group of mature Ethiopian evangelical Christians had been formed, the Swedish Mission had very wisely handed the running of the church over to the indigenous believers. This was a lovely outcome of a faithful missionary work.

I was sure the Lord would have the boys fellowship

with the local indigenous church in Addis Ababa, as well as having their fellowship meetings at the school. It was important that they were identified as members of the body of Christ, expressed in membership of the local church.

Later, when I had moved to Eritrea, I had very encouraging letters from most of them. Abainekh wrote that the group in the school had grown to twenty-five, and included Ma'irgo who had moved to Wingate.[4]

In May 1955 whilst in Aden, I met some SIM missionaries from Ethiopia. They told me that the meetings of the Wingate believers were continuing. Prefects had stopped them having meetings but they had appealed to the Director of the School, and he had granted them permission to continue.

---

4. David Stokes later moved to Gondar, and a number of the Wingate boys went to Gondar to work or to study. David took them under his wing, and wrote the following letter to me. This was a token of the Lord's continuing care for them.

7/12/1955.
Dear Bev,
It was a delight to get your letter, forwarded on by Caroline from Gondar.... 'Masfin, Mamo, Bellaga, and Tedassa' – these are 'yours', are they? I'd like to know, Bev, just the ones in which you are specially interested. Masfin, of course, is grand, and a brother. He has needed help, for he has a beautifully tender conscience, and so he passed through one *most* difficult phase, but now, thank God, he is well on top again. Mamo is still a bit 'light' and unreliable, he needs more ballast. Bellaga is a nice boy, quite settled I think; he's younger than the others. Tedassa is a good lad, confirmed and settled, and now accompanies Masfin and me to the prison – preaching on

7

The Mustard Seed Flourishing in Ethiopia

From the end of December 1953 to the middle of January 1954, Lionel was showing Ed Marquart around our prospective Fields on the African Side, as well as some of the Lord's work in Ethiopia. They had a trip out to Fichee and the BCMS Bible College there. Ed was also invited to visit the SIM Revival area in the Cambatta Tribe at Soddu, and was deeply impressed with what he saw and experienced.

A few days later, Ed flew across to Aden to meet Jack, Kath and Marion, and to see the Field on that side of the Red Sea. They had had a Field Council meeting while Ed was there and he returned to Addis with minutes of that meeting, including its conclusions. Lionel and I were very grieved with the minutes, subject matter and conclusions. The enemy was at work seeking to bring division.

We had an Ethiopian Field Council meeting on 21st-22nd January, involving Lionel, Ed and myself. All points and differences were frankly discussed; then there was a time of real getting through in prayer, and indeed into a real unity in the Spirit. It was only then that the issues became clear and what decisions we

---

Sundays. They all come, of course, to the Sunday morning meeting and very frequently visit our house.

I was glad to see how the Lord has been guiding in your affairs, keep us informed, and tell us when Li comes!

All greetings to you in our Lord,
David.

should make. The effort and the concentration, at this time, should be on the Danakil side. Jack and Marion, I knew by their letters, were grieved, but the Lord graciously overruled the differences and bound us into a real Team, an instrument in his hand, for his work in the Red Sea area.

Lionel felt that we should start in Eritrean Danakil, which was without any witness. It was decided that he and Ed should travel to Asmara and see what the prospects were for openings in Eritrea. From there, they were continuing on to Egypt, and then to the USA, Canada and Britain for deputation work.

Lionel thought that after finishing the first language exam I should go to Eritrea and get notes on the Danakil language from Frances Mahuffy. Frances worked with Clarence Duff and was well trained in Wycliffe Linguistics. He had spent some time in the Danakil and had compiled some valuable notes on the language. Lionel instructed me to put in an application for permission to open mission stations in the Danakil. I should also apply for a resident's visa. This had to be applied for while in the country, but could not be granted to one holding a visitor's visa, which meant I would then have to leave the country. Lionel thought that I should go back to Aden and help Jack until the resident's visa was granted. It seemed that this was of the Lord, as it worked out exactly as he had visualized.

Lionel and Ed left for Asmara on Monday, 25th January 1954. It was just over two years before I was to see Lionel again, although we kept in close touch by mail all the time.

The Missions, and Inter-Mission Relationships

The oldest mission was, I think, *The Swedish Mission* and their areas were mainly Western Ethiopia and Eritrea. In the early days, some of their missionaries were martyred. Their policy had been to put their converts into the Coptic Church, but that Church had reacted against them and rejected the converts. The Mission then established indigenous churches, mostly in the west, and there had been revival in these churches which was still continuing.

The Sudan Interior Mission (SIM) was the largest mission in Ethiopia. The work was founded by Dr. Lambie, who had felt the call to Ethiopia when he was with the United Presbyterian Mission in Sudan. At that time he could not enter Ethiopia. Later, after being in Ethiopia, Alfred Buxton had gone to the USA and spoken with Dr. Lambie and they agreed to found a mission to Ethiopia. This did not materialize, so Dr. Lambie accepted the backing of SIM to open a work. During an exploratory trek with an early pioneering team, Dr. Lambie travelled into the Cambatta and Wallamo tribes. As a result, they received permission to open mission stations in these tribal areas. One of those who had been on the trek with Dr. Lambie was Clarence Duff. Clarence had helped pioneer the work in one of these two tribes and we learned from him an account of how wonderfully God worked.

By the time the Italians invaded Ethiopia in 1956, there were about thirty weak converts in each of the two tribes. The missionaries felt that the Roman Catholic Church would press the army to expel them, and that they should give the converts as much Bible instruction as possible in the time that was left. After about half a year the missionaries were expelled, and there was no news of these converts[1] for six years until missionaries returned after Ethiopia was liberated.

Meanwhile, through the Holy Spirit, the Lord Jesus was doing something very wonderful. The believers only had a few Scripture portions in their tribal languages. A few had Amharic Bibles. When they met at first they were bewildered, their human props had been removed. Then problems arose and they would not know what to do. One would think of a Bible verse, but as they thought and prayed about it, they would realize that it was not applicable, so other suggested verses would be considered. Then one would suggest a Scripture that came to his mind, and if there was a general recognition that this was the Lord's answer, then it would be acted upon. In this way, their work, their churches and church order were built up step by step on the Word of God applied by the Holy Spirit.

When the missionaries came back, they found that God had done a wonderful thing in both tribes. There were about 30,000 Christians in each, with New Testament churches experiencing revival blessing. Tribes' people were being converted, added to the churches, being built up in sound doctrine, and giving themselves unconditionally to the Lord for his service. They were being sent forth in pairs by their local churches to other

1. Mrs. Mollie McKenzie knew of some elderly lady missionaries in the USA who had been burdened to pray several hours a day for the weak converts.

villages and tribes, and being upheld by prayer and sacrificial giving. The gospel and revival were spreading like fire. The Coptic Church leaders were pressing local governors to try to stamp out the work. Believers and their families were being arrested and imprisoned, and their churches burned down, but the fire in their hearts was burning only brighter.

At the time I was in Addis, the American Ambassador Mr. Simonsen, a godly man and an ordained minister, was a great help. All the persecution was carried out without the Emperor's knowledge. Sometimes, as a last resort, some would go to Mr. Simonsen and give him the facts about some persecution. He had access to the Emperor, who, when he heard of the matter, would immediately take effective steps to put an end to the injustices.

When Ed went to Soddu in the Cambatta area, he was deeply impressed with what he saw. He said that the missionaries did not come back as lords over God's heritage, but as examples to the flock, as fellow helpers of their joy.

However, Satan had been working on the leaders and elders of the churches. They, simple men just a few years before, had come to have sway over multitudes and were becoming drunk with power and puffed up with pride. God had then been graciously humbling them, bringing them low before himself and undoing the destroying work of Satan.

This was an object lesson to me on the true aim and method of missionary work. It should not be to bring converts into our denominational organizations, under some hierarchy or control of leaders or councils in a foreign country. We are the Lord's scaffolding for him to use in building his church. Through the gospel, he brings sinners to repentance and to faith in himself. He wants them to be brought together in local fellowships and to be built up by them, individually and collectively, being in a living communication and relationship with himself by his Holy Spirit. That is being under the heavenly Jerusalem, the heavenly seat of authority, by the Holy Spirit (Heb. 12:22-29). We are not to take the place of the Holy Spirit and bind the believers in our man-made, well-meaning organizations, which become an end in themselves. In this way we hinder and grieve the Holy Spirit, so that he leaves us to it. This results in a proliferation of dead religious bodies with no, or very little, sign of vital, victorious spiritual life. 'The body without the Spirit is dead.' I believe that coming into contact with these operations of the Holy Spirit was part of his very necessary preparation of us as a Team to be a collection of his building scaffolding.

The American United Presbyterians had an extensive work: hospitals, clinics, schools and churches.

The Mennonites had a very fine School for the Blind in Addis Ababa, with a good team of Ethiopian believers as teachers. A number of the blind pupils were finding Christ at the school. The Emperor often visited the school and was deeply interested in it. On his travels, if he saw a blind child, he would arrange for that child to be sent to the school. When the Mennonites would protest that they were absolutely full, he would arrange for an allocation of funds for them to extend.

The Norwegian Mission had been expelled from China in 1951, and had received permission from the Emperor to be redeployed in the far south of Ethiopia, towards the Kenya border. They had about forty missionaries in the country. Some years later, we rejoiced to hear that through some of the Cambatta or Wallamo evangelists, the fire of revival was spreading in their area also.

The Pentecostal Finnish Mission was a small mission led by Mr. and Mrs. Madsen, a warm hearted, elderly couple.

BCMS had a very fine team led by David and Caroline Stokes. At Fichee, north of Addis Ababa, was a men's and a women's Bible School. Many, if not most, of the national believers working with other missions had been trained in this Bible School. David kept in touch with most of the ex-students through a news sheet and personal correspondence.

One of the BCMS staff, Mike Blair, had graduated at Cambridge, where he had continued in agricultural research. He had been converted at Cambridge through Rev. Ronald Adeney, who we came to know well later in Israel. Mike joined BCMS in 1947 and established a Mission farm at Soudee in the Arusi province. A wealthy Ethiopian lady allocated the land to BCMS for this purpose. The idea was for it to be a centre for evangelism to three nearby population centres. The aim was for converts to take over the running of it later, as Mike would seek to pioneer another such farm elsewhere. A number of the Bible School pupils went there in vacation time to help and to earn grain for their support for the next term at the Bible School.

I could understand that the Lord might want to use BCMS as his instrument for bringing light and life to the Coptic Church, or even for some of the Bible School students to be called of God to enter the Coptic Church as a field of witness. However, I could not see that the Lord would have them put new converts, babes in Christ, into such a Church, as a matter of policy. What sort of food would they be nourished with? Is it right to put live babies among the dead, or dying? They need spiritual milk or meat, not deadening poison.

I personally believe that the idea of national churches is not according to God's plan, as he reveals it in the building of the early church. We see a universal church consisting of only true believers, the body of Christ, expressed geographically in local churches. All of these are to be directly under the Holy Spirit, who alone can give true unity, rather than man-made uniformity. We see in Scripture that younger churches can be used of the Lord to be an inspiration to the older churches. The older churches should be able to give help and counsel to the younger churches, as they seek the mind of the Spirit on problems.

The Church Mission to the Jews (CMJ) is an Anglican Mission and was working in the Gondar area among the Falasha Jews. There had been martyrs among the Falashas in the early days. It was an evangelical work, but they, too, had the policy of putting their converts into the Coptic Church.

Inter-Mission Relationships

There was a very good relationship between the various missions. I believe that one of the main reasons for this was a weekly, united prayer meeting in Addis, very similar to the one in Aden. One of the practices at BCMS, too, was a great blessing, and that was a 'Quiet Day' once a month. All work was put aside, and we usually went without breakfast and lunch.

The Coptic Church

Our Norwegian friend, Mr. Bredvej of Mosvolds, very kindly took Lionel and me, with some others, to Lake Zukwala to witness the celebration of the annual Baptism, called Timqat. Similar celebrations were taking place at holy places all over the country. This lake was in the crater of an extinct volcano. On the rim of the crater was a Coptic Church and Monastery. As the Scriptures and their services had for centuries been in the dead Geez language, their customs, practices and beliefs had gone very far from the Word of God. There is something from the Old and the New Testaments in them, but the main teaching in their Churches is based on fables and legends.

There are many stories of Tekla Haimanaut (who may have been a very live evangelical Christian). It was said of him that he ploughed Ethiopia with the gospel. However, all that is taught of him nowadays is certainly not of the Holy Spirit. The reason Lake Zukwala was revered as a holy site was because Tekla Haimanaut stood on one leg in the middle of the lake for one year praying. Another of the stories is that on one occasion he continued praying while ravens were

81

pecking his eyes out. Then there was one of the cannibal who had eaten twelve men; but one day he gave a cup of cold water to a beggar, so he was all right, he could go to heaven. These and many more fabulous stories are told and depicted in paintings on the walls in their Churches.

The paintings are of a very simple, almost juvenile style, with most of the characters shown full-faced or side-faced. The ones shown full-faced are the good ones, they can look you in the eyes; but the side-faced are the bad ones. Also, the ones painted with the lighter skin are the good ones and those with the darker colour are the bad ones.

A very high proportion of the males are priests or monks. The younger ones are each draped in a sheep's fleece. Their maintenance comes largely from saying prayers for the souls of people after death, so as to reduce their sufferings and time in purgatory. Consequently, when a man dies, a number of priests, monks and student priests descend on the house and for some days eat the poor widow out of house and home. It is in such countries that the words of the Bible really become alive. 'They go about in sheep's clothing, but inwardly they are ravening wolves...' 'They devour widows' houses, and for a pretence make long prayers.'

Their Churches are nearly all octagonal in shape. A central octagon is the most holy place, a second octagon surrounding it is the holy place for the priests, and the outer octagon for the congregation.

When we arrived at the Monastery, a very large crowd had already gathered, waiting for the celebrations to begin. Eventually, the priests and monks emerged, some leading and carrying the 'Ark,' which, I understand, is a block of wood covered with brightly coloured velvet. Most of the priests were carrying brightly coloured and multi-coloured umbrellas.

The crowds all joined behind the procession, wending its way down to the lake side. Lionel was delighted to find that the service included a reading from Luke's Gospel in Amharic. This was evidence of the Emperor's long and faithful struggle to get Amharic used in the Churches. It was strongly resisted by the very conservative hierarchy. However, more and more Churches were going over to Amharic. The closing part of the celebration was the actual 'baptism.' Most of the priests were carrying horse-hair switches, something like round, very long-haired paintbrushes.

Several of the senior priests went to the water's edge and kept dipping their switches into the water of the lake, which during the proceedings had been 'blessed' by the priest. This 'holy' water was then sprinkled over the crowd, the switches being continually dipped, and flicked over them. The faithful were milling around, trying to get within range of the drops, and all making a warbling sound by moving the forefinger around inside rounded lips, while voicing a high pitched note. If a few drops landed on them, they could move out of the crowd, having received their baptism(?) for the year.

They probably imagined that they had had their spiritual cleansing, sufficient to last until the next Timqat. The 'T' and 'q' are actually plosive letters, and we do not have this type of consonant in English, nor any other language I know of.

After the ceremony, the accepted custom throughout the country was for the priests and monks to return to the monastery and to get blind drunk on native Tej, a beer made by fermenting bread, and also a very potent drink made by fermenting honey. It seemed so depressing, having a celebration with such a curiously twisted and changed idea of scriptural baptism, and then to finish it with something absolutely condemned in God's Word: 'Be not deceived .... neither,... drunkards, shall inherit the Kingdom of God."

The administration
I spent about two months trying to get a three months extension of visa, firstly going almost every day to the Foreign Ministry for several hours a day, and later doing the same thing at the Ministry of the Interior.

The administration was ponderous and unwieldy, not so much because of the officials themselves, who were very gentlemanly, polite and highly intelligent, but because they were badly in need of experienced help and advice for establishing an efficient workable system.

For example, a driving license could be obtained at any time of the year, but was only valid until 31st December. There was an office open to receive applications all the year round, but for the next year it had to be applied for as commencing from 1st

January. This meant that there were enormous queues for about two weeks, after which the staff had very little to do for the rest of the year. If one had a license, but then did not renew it, for say ten years, a new license would only be issued if the fee for the ten intervening years was also paid.

Ethiopia was emerging from medieval feudalism into a modern society, but was handicapped by a very high rate of illiteracy. The Emperor had done much for his country, not least in raising educational standards, but he was faced with an enormous task.

When the British Army liberated Ethiopia from the Italian occupation, and the Emperor returned to Addis Ababa on 5th May 1941, the British were held in high esteem. Also, they had granted asylum to the Emperor in Britain during his exile. Britain decided to help the country, which had very big, undeveloped resources. Presumably, in order to safeguard its investments, they pressed for a British Administration of the country for at least ten years. Immediately the Emperor and the Ethiopian Leaders reacted vehemently – they were sure that the motives were purely imperialistic – and absolutely refused. They invited neutral nations to help in various ways, such as inviting Sweden to help build up their Air Force.

Many expected a massacre of Italians after the war, but the Emperor forbade any such excesses. Consequently, many Italians stayed on in the country and provided many of the skills and crafts that were a great help. They, the invaders, won the respect that eluded the liberators. Even by 1953 Britain still had a very bad name. Pure motives, wisdom and tact would have saved such a reversal. Help from Britain in development, and a sharing of experience in administration, could have been of immense benefit to Ethiopia. The story in Eritrea was quite different, as I was to see later.

Meanwhile, Russia was beginning to build up an influence in the country. In 1953, the Russian Embassy had a staff of about 400; far, far bigger than was required to represent their country in Ethiopia. It was the centre for communist propaganda for all of Africa, and in that continent there was plenty of inflammatory material that could be set alight. Every teacher in Ethiopia received each month a large amount of beautifully coloured, printed communist propaganda in Amharic.[2]

The country was 50% Coptic Christian; the other 50% being mostly Muslim, with some Pagan. The Coptic Church was ill-equipped spiritually to meet the incoming flood of atheism. I could see a tremendous missionary responsibility and challenge for the area resting on the Lord's people labouring there, as well as on the whole Church of Christ.

The Lord's timing and provision were perfect. Several things happened to indicate this.

First, just as my language course was coming to a close, I had word that Elsa was on her way out from Canada.

Then, just three weeks before taking the language

---

2. Soviet strategy did result in a communist takeover of the country for a number of years.

exams, Mr. Ashley, the Agent for the Bible Society, had heard that I would be going to Eritrea. He told me that he and his wife would be travelling to Asmara in the Microbus about 8th May and that it should be possible for them to take me with them. What a wonderful Lord we serve!

We had our language exams on 30th April, and the next day I heard that I was second with 80%, and Alister Frazer of BCMS had soared ahead with 93%. Elsa arrived unexpectedly the same day and had had an awful job finding BCMS. The Lord helped wonderfully, for she met some of her old students who escorted her to BCMS. I was able to hand the mission accounts over to Elsa. She had come out at the age of fifty-six into a faith work, in pioneer fields, and to stand behind us at the Addis Ababa Joint Headquarters with BCMS, for the advance into Danakil.

Mr. Ashley confirmed that he would be able to take me, and as they did not have much luggage they would be able to take a good deal of mine and Lionel's. There was not much difficulty in getting a permit to travel to Eritrea as my visa was in order.

Third, I had written to Mr. Frances Mahaffy in Senafay, Eritrea, and he had invited me to stay with him for a few days to go over his Danakil language notes, for which I was deeply grateful.

8

To Eritrea - for Danakil

As promised Mr. and Mrs. Ashley took me with them to Asmara. We left Addis on 8th May 1954. The Lord's provision was again amazing. They had removed the middle seat of the Microbus so I managed to take all our great load of luggage another three days of the journey. Mr. Ashley was a bit taken back, but he was quite gracious about it. We camped for the night near Debra Sena.

The following day, Sunday, we went on to Dessaye. It was a tough ride from Cambulcha but there were some wonderfully engineered mountain roads. One good thing the Italian occupation had done for Ethiopia was in laying these main trunk roads which had opened up the country a great deal. Passing through Dessaye, we went through Argo to an SIM Leper Colony. Torrential rain started so we decided to stay the night at a hotel. The next day was an amazing journey with tremendous changes of climate. A number of times we descended to 3,000ft., then up to 8,000, then down to the desert at sea level, and then up to 10,000ft. Many of the roads were very steep, with forty or more hairpin bends in a climb or descent.

We stopped at the SIM Mission in Mai Chow, where we were invited to supper and to stay the night. We had lovely Christian fellowship with Miss Joyce Paxton, Miss Vi Swanson, and the Davenports. The next day we set off on the final leg of our journey.

With the Mahaffy family in Senafay

We reached Senafay at 6 pm. There were two families there, the Mahaffys and the Birds; they belonged to the Mission of a small, very fundamental, American Presbyterian Church group. The Ashleys stayed with the Birds, and I with the Mahaffys. The next morning, I settled my share of the expenses of the journey with Mr. Ashley. They went on to Asmara while I stayed on with the Mahaffys.

Mr. Mahaffy had taken the full course of Wycliffe Linguistics. He had prepared eighty pages of typescript on the Danakil language; so far as is known, it was the only existing material, apart from some notes of Lionel, in this otherwise unwritten language. So all that day I was steeped in a new and strange terminology of phonemes, subject indicators, tensed pharyngeal vocalized fricatives, etc. A common 'P' sounds strange when called 'a bilabial vocalized plosive'. This nomenclature is part of a very scientific and very effective approach to the breaking down, analysis, formulation of grammar, accidence, syntax and vocabularies of unwritten languages.

At one stage the Mahaffy family had set up a base in Danakil, but the difficulties had been enormous. The place, they found, was a hotbed of brigand (called Shifta) activity. They were threatened by them but firmly resisted moving. However, Mr. Mahaffy was stricken with a strange eye disease. It almost ruined the sight of one eye, and somewhat impaired the vision of the other. On top of everything, several members of the family were literally at death's door with malignant malaria. The mission insisted that they move to another area. They were moved to Senafay in the hill country, with not so fierce a climate, among the Saho tribe. This was a neighbouring and a cousin tribe to the Danakil. I believe that their language, too, was an unwritten one. Mr. Mahaffy gave me one of the few existing copies of his Danakil notes.

I learned from Mr. Mahaffy that all the languages that were broken down were found to have an intelligent, meaningful, grammar structure. The natives speak grammatically, yet people picking up the language simply murder the grammar, like people speaking pigeon English. Language is another amazing manifestation of the divine intelligence we find in creation.

I also learned from Mr. Mahaffy that there is a rich folklore among the Danakil people, and their stories are recounted over and over again. Many of the stories were of the Hyena and the Jackal. The Hyena being the big, strong but stupid type of character, continually outwitted by the weaker but cunning Jackal. However, on occasions the Hyena has the laugh, as the Jackal falls victim to his own craftiness. Many other stories are of the Sham man (a Damascus man, or Syrian), and the Yemeny man. These stories, unwritten and passed on only by word of mouth, show a shrewd appraisal of character and insight into attitudes and relationships of people.

Asmara

On Thursday 13th May, Mr. Mahaffy was going to Asmara, so he very kindly took me with him. We went to the SIM Rest Home in the outskirts of Asmara, a section called 'Paradiso' – Paradise! Mr. and Mrs. Ashley were there and had arranged with the Emmels for me to stay.

On the following day I went with Mr. Ashley to the Swedish Mission in Asmara. We called to see Mrs. Winquist. At the age of 90, she was engaged in the task of translating the Bible into the Tigrinia language. She was proof reading about four to six hours a day and was up to the book of Isaiah. She asked which mission I was with. I told her that I was with Dr. Gurney. 'Oh!' she said, 'I am praying much for him, I have a great burden for the Muslim people. Where is Marion Thomas now?' It showed her deep prayerful interest.

Many of the Eritrean leaders, including the Governor of Eritrea, had been educated in the Swedish Mission Schools. The Mission was held in high esteem in the country.

Mr. Ashley very kindly took me on very interesting trip to Keren. This had been an Italian stronghold and could only be taken by direct frontal attack. When General Platt's two Indian divisions took it in March 1941, they suffered 3,000 casualties. Its fall broke Italian power in Eritrea.

At Keren we went to see Pastor and Mrs. Olle Hagner of the Swedish Mission. They had given a lifetime of service for the Lord in Eritrea, mostly with the Cunama tribe. Mr. Ashley was seeing to the publication by the Bible Society of a new edition of the Cunama New Testament, translated by Mr. Hagner. The Hagners were going out to their station at Kulluku in Cunama the next day. They kindly invited us to stay with them overnight, and then to accompany them to Kulluku for a few days. We very gladly accepted.

This was Mrs. Hagner's homecoming to Cunama, after being away in Sweden for seventeen years for the education of the children. Meanwhile Pastor Hagner had faithfully laboured among the people for whom the Lord had had them commit their lives.

As we approached Kulluku, we saw men and women of the Cunama tribe, a Nilotic tribe (of the Nile). They were very black and seemed very wild and primitive. The men had spears, wore a very small loin cloth, and some had bones in their noses, some beads, and a short dagger. Many of the women had little on below the waist, while some were completely naked.

Kulluku was a village of about 300, with 60 Christians. What a contrast to see the Christians, the ladies with nice dresses and the men with shirts and shorts. They came out with tremendous joy to meet dear Mrs. Hagner, hugging and kissing her, with tears of joy. She was just overwhelmed,

Mr. Ashley spoke on the work of the Bible Society, and gave them a slogan, 'Each one, teach one!' They then sang a chorus, 'Each one, teach one' – they made it up on the spot. Then Esaias, one of the leaders, gave a lovely speech of welcome and said that they were going to have a collection for the Bible Society. Different ones spoke and others interpreted. I was just overjoyed to sense the deep spirituality of these dear people.

It is tragic that churches so often become places for permanent, passive pew-sitters, spiritual refrigerators, to preserve the faithful for heaven. They should rather be ovens where the bread of life is produced to bring eternal life to those throughout the world who are under a sentence of eternal death. True Christianity is Christ in us, reproducing his own life of sacrificial love in us, and through us in others.

Mr. Hagner had produced a reading primer in Cunama in Romanized script. He had put in some very interesting Cunama folklore stories.

We left on Friday 21st May and the dear Christians presented me with a hand embroidered table cloth in their own style as a keepsake of my visit to them.

Application for Danakil

On Saturday 22nd May, I went to the Immigration Office to see Ato Samuel, the Director, who was very friendly and helpful. He seemed well informed on missions. He knew English well, and spoke about Alfred Buxton and asked about David Stokes. Lionel had put in an application to start mission work, but Ato Samuel advised me to put in another application, and also how to draft it. He said that I should apply for a resident's visa and meanwhile to apply for an extension of my tourist visa.

Mr. Ashley kindly let me use his typewriter to type out the application for the Red Sea Mission Team to open up Mission Stations in Danakil. Permission for a headquarters in Asmara and a forwarding base in Massawa was included in the application. I also applied for my tourist visa extension and for a resident's visa. On Tuesday, I went in to see Ato Samuel; again he was extremely friendly and granted me a three months extension of my tourist visa on the spot. It went into the archives there and then, and within half an hour the visa was in my passport. He said he would see that the other applications went forward.

I was amazed at the difference in the administrative procedure between Eritrea and Ethiopia. The British administered Eritrea for ten years under a mandate from the United Nations. At first they continued using Italian officials, gradually replacing them by Britons. But they did something that was praiseworthy; they appointed Eritreans to understudy all the administrative posts. This meant that when Eritrea eventually voted to be federated with Ethiopia, they had a trained and experienced national administration to run the country. Also, the Eritreans are a highly intelligent people.

Ato Samuel had advised me not to return immediately to Aden. He said that it would complicate matters, but it was only later that I understood why. However, I took it as the Lord's leading, especially as I had had a warm invitation from Bud and Dot Acord to stay with them while seeking the entry into Danakil. Bud and Dot, who had been with the SIM in Aden, were now in charge of the SIM Station in Assab. From later experience I think that the advice not to return to Aden, but to wait for the permits to come through, enabled the authorities to investigate me before granting the permits. This, they could do wherever I was in the country, but not if I went abroad. At the time I had peace about it. As events turned out, it was surely the Lord's prepared way.

On to Assab

I flew to Assab on Friday 28th May. Bud and Dot were there to meet me and gave me a lovely warm welcome. That evening they had a games night in their house. There were Arabs, Danakil, Italians, Amharas and an Indian; it was very good.

The next day Bud took me to see Sheikh Musa Ga'as, the District Officer, whom I had met on my previous visit to Assab. He was very pleased that we wanted to start a work for his people. He spoke English fairly well, but he wanted to improve it, and asked if I would help him, and he would help me to learn Danakil. He became a key figure in our getting an entrance into the Danakil.

We also went to see Ato Chanlau, the Chief Secretary to His Majesty's Representative in Assab, Col. Legassa. He, too, was extremely friendly and also was to play an important part in our obtaining the openings into the Danakil.

Bud and Dot knew a young man, Hussein, who spoke Arabic and Danakil. He agreed to work with us as a house boy and language informant. I tried to spend as much time as I could on the Afar language.

One of the Ethiopian young men I had contact with, Tekaba, professed to be a Christian, but admitted that he had not been born again. He was very responsive and asked Christ to come into his heart on the basis of his promise in Revelation 3:20. Dot told me the next day that Tekaba had said to her that he had received Christ. There was evidence later that the grace of the Lord was working in his life. It was the beginning of another of the Lord's 'chain reactions'.

He worked in the Post Office and somehow had permission to sleep and eat at the Army Camp. He started bringing the Captain, Lieutenant and others from the Camp, and also some from the Post Office, to the meetings and English classes. Mamo, from the Post Office, began to take a keen interest in spiritual things. After a Saturday Bible class, he asked how we could know if we are saved. He put his faith in the Lord Jesus that night. Later, he told me that he had the assurance that the Lord Jesus had received him.

Bud and Dot left on holiday on 26th June, leaving me in charge of the house and their work.

Ato Chanlau came sometimes to the Bible classes and the English classes. On one occasion he seemed quite touched by the message and said that he would come more often and that we must talk together on spiritual things. He seemed rather shy, but a very wise, capable and sincere type of person.

For most of my time in Assab, I had the distinct impression that I was being investigated. My incoming and outgoing mail was seven to ten days longer than for others, I think this was part of the process of vetting me for my resident's permit and our mission application. Later, a letter from Ato Chanlau to the authorities, reporting that I was cleared and recognized as a known friend, tipped the scales, when later the question of our acceptance was in the balance.

Sometimes when Sheik Musa Ga'as came we spoke on spiritual things. I suggested getting him a New Testament in basic English and he agreed, so I sent to Aden for one. When he came on Wednesday 7th July, he told me that a police truck was going on a trip for about three days into Danakil territory, in the region of 'Edd. He said that he could arrange for me to go with them. Of course I jumped at the chance. I showed him a copy of our application to open up work in Eritrea. When he saw the word 'Evangelistic', he said, 'Ah! So you are going to fight against my religion, Eh!' Later, he did say that spiritual things were important and that we must discuss them sometime. He could not understand why we could not accept their 'prophet'.

I then went to see Ato Chanlau and showed him our application. He asked about our mission and how we got our funds. He said that he could give me a visa extension and also a re-entry visa if I went to Aden. Somehow I missed getting this re-entry visa. It would have saved a long delay in getting back from Aden, after the resident's visa was granted. I did not understand this at the time, but as it turned out later, the Lord's timing was perfect through the delay caused by not getting the re-entry visa.

9

Stranded in Danakil

I went to see Lieutenant Abdullah, a Saho, who was in charge of the police lorry that was going into Danakil. He was definitely not keen on my going. It was only when I agreed to give him a signed letter saying that he had no responsibility for me whatsoever, that he was willing to take me. We were to start the next afternoon, Friday 9th July.

The lorry was a Chevrolet four-wheeled-drive truck, loaded with sacks of grain and other supplies for a police outpost at Bellabuwee. There had been a series of lootings and murders in the area and this temporary outpost had been set up to try to capture the perpetrators of these crimes.

The driver, Mr. Thompson was an African from Gold Coast who spoke English quite well. Seated next to him in front was Lieutenant Abdullah. In the back the others were seated or sprawled on sacks of grain, with no shade from the sun. Two were policemen: Esa (Jesus, in Arabic), a Danakil, and Tewaldy, a Tigray-speaking, Coptic Christian. In addition to myself there were two Danakil passengers from 'Edd. We set off at about 4.30 pm, and reached Beilul, sixty kilometres away, by about 7 pm. It was a permanent Danakil coastal village, surrounded by a large area of Dome Palm, evidence of a plentiful supply of good water. The Danakil make cone cups of the leaves, and they tap the branches, collecting the drippings of the sap in these cups. It is a very potent, alcoholic drink, but in about thirty-six hours it turns to a very good vinegar. Although Islam condemns alcohol, I was told that practically all the villagers were drunk by about ten each morning.

Shortly after we left Beilul, we were overtaken by a convoy of Locust Control people. They had two Land Rovers and two Dodge Power Wagons.

It was soon obvious that our driver was intoxicated. After some time, he stopped the lorry and got out, vomiting violently, after which he seemed to sober up somewhat. From shortly after Assab there was no proper road, although as far as Beilul it was a beaten track. From then on we were just driving over open country, the driver picking the best way he could. By 10 pm we arrived at Wadi, a water hole, where we camped for the night. I did not take their advice to fill my canteen there. It seemed no time before we were up, at 5.30 am. I found the water was quite brown and was so glad that I had not polluted the good water in my canteen. And I could not help but think of guinea worm contamination.

At Beilul we had picked up Ahmed Yasseen, who was from 'Edd, and worked in Assab. He was a nephew of Sheik Musa Ga'as. About noon we arrived at 'Edd, which is on the coast, about 220 kilometres north of Assab. We were in a lather of perspiration and covered with dust. There were about eighty huts, the frames of which were of acacia wood, with palm leaf matting for walls and roof covering. They were built on the soft sand, with the same sandy floor inside. We were invited into the compound, containing a number of houses, of Haj Yasseen, Ahmed's father. Haj is an honorary title of one who has been on the Haj, or pilgrimage, to Mecca. Ahmed's mother was Sheik Musa's sister.

We were received very courteously. They produced water, soap and towel for me to wash in a separate room, so I was able to change. There was then a very big meal for us.

We set off at 4 pm for Bellabuwee, striking west. It was very dusty and very hard going for the lorry. We got really stuck in the soft sand so they decided to camp the night there. The next morning, not long after we set off, the Locust Control people passed us again, this time in the opposite direction. We arrived at Bellabuwee at 10 am, it is about 80 kilometres from 'Edd. There was just one permanent house and a well of good water. The police post was on a small hill, which commanded quite a large area. Lieutenant Ibrahim was in charge, and he had with him a sergeant and eight other policemen.

We were faced with a very big problem. Thompson told me that the dynamo had not been charging since we had camped the night at Wadi. That meant we had been running on the battery, and when it was discharged we would be stranded. It seemed incredible that a driver would just keep going in such circumstances. Furthermore, it was culpable negligence that he had let the Locust Control people pass without seeking help from them. Such negligence could easily cost lives.

The next morning, some went with the truck to the well to get water. I pleaded with them to start the engine with the hand crank.

We set off about 6.30 am, taking a few passengers, including a Danakil hunter. On the way, they spotted a deer, so the hunter borrowed Tewaldy's rifle, and went stalking it down wind. He used three bullets but missed. The truck started off and the hunter had to run like the wind to catch up. When he got in the truck, he was examining his instep. He tried to extract a thorn with a crude brass tweezer he carried on a string around his neck.

Then began a chain of events that I believe the Lord used to open Danakil to us. I asked if I could help and he agreed. I got out my first aid kit in which I had a darning needle. Within a few minutes, I had speared the thorn, and managed to lever it out; it was about ¾" long, and had gone straight in. What amazed me was that he had shown no sign of a limp as he had raced to the truck. My having the first aid kit, and getting the thorn out so quickly, really impressed them. Anyway, the hunter was very grateful, and I put some iodine on it, and a dressing, with plaster.

After some time the battery showed signs that it was nearing exhaustion. Somehow we managed to stagger into 'Edd. Thompson and I removed the dynamo, but it was ruined. Haj Yasseen was our host and provided accommodation and food, but it was obvious that he was not happy about having to care for five strangers indefinitely.

A 'Hakeem'?
It seems that because of removing the thorn and of having a little first aid kit, I was, quite erroneously,

reputed as a big 'Hakeem', literally, 'a wise one', but commonly used for a doctor. Ahmed Yasseen said that there was a woman who was very sick and asked if I could help her. She was the favourite wife of Ibrahim, a shark hunter. I questioned them, but I am afraid that my poor Arabic, especially in medical and health terms, led me off track. What I gathered was that she had had a stillborn baby twenty days previously, but her abdomen was still very distended. It seemed that the afterbirth had come away, but she had been constipated for three weeks. I asked if they had any 'English' salts (Epsom salts), but they hadn't.

The next morning, Haj Yasseen came to me, asking if I could do anything for his foot. He had a nasty abscess and said he could not sleep for the pain. I treated it with hot fomentations and dressed it with boracic lint and boracic powder.

Ibrahim came and asked me about his wife. Being a chemist, I reckoned that table salt should also draw water into the bowels. I told them to dissolve a teaspoonful of salt in a glass of water, for her to sip. They should give her about three such glasses a day. Through my inadequate Arabic and wrong diagnosis, I found out later that what I had prescribed would actually worsen her condition.

The next day Haj Yasseen came again to have his foot dressed. He was very grateful and said he had had the first good night's sleep for sometime.

Igahali, a Danakil policeman, asked me about a disease that many of them had. I could tell from the description that it was Guinea Worm. I had learned about this from Lionel and had also read up about it.

I told them that it is caused by drinking infected water, usually at a well, or water hole. The embryos develop in a tiny, secondary host. It takes twelve months for the worms to mature in the human body. The male is about seven centimetres long, and the female about thirty centimetres. They find each other and mate. The female is able to discharge her eggs by dissolving part of the skin of an arm or leg when the limb is immersed in water. There is a way of getting the female out by pulling the protruding tail end out, an inch a day. When they try to pull it all out, as they always do, the worm breaks, and they get a terrible abscess, filled with about a cup of pus.

I was able to tell them how to prevent getting infected by boiling, or simply filtering, drinking water through muslin and then boiling or destroying the muslin. I told them also how to extract the female without breaking it.

They were all really delighted to get this information about Guinea Worm. I was sure the Lord would use this, for they would spread this important news far and wide. He would show them how much we could help them in so many ways and use it to break down the opposition to our acceptance.

In the evening Ibrahim came again. He was very worried about his wife because it seemed that the salt was not doing any good. Thompson was with me so with his help in interpretation, the real facts came to light. Her bowels were all right and had been all the time. He said that what had not come away was the blood. On questioning him, I understood that the water had come away and the placenta, but he kept insisting that it was the blood that had not come away. It seemed that his other wife had had a severe haemorrhage. Her abdomen was still very swollen, as were her arms, legs and face. I told them that I had had a completely wrong picture. I asked if I could see his wife, and to this he agreed.

She was sitting on the ground, moaning and swooning. I told Ibrahim that she must lie down and not be sitting on the floor as she had been, and that she should have nourishing meat soups. He said that he would attend to these things. When I further questioned him, he affirmed that when she tried to stand, she could not, she was too dizzy. As her bowels were normal I told them to stop giving her salt.

The next morning, I awoke about 4.30 and could not get back to sleep. So I decided to go to the beach to have a Quiet Time there.

After a while I saw beams of light over the escarpment inland, then the lights of two cars became visible. They were descending towards the coast, but at an angle that would miss 'Edd. I ran as fast as I could to try to intercept them before they turned north, parallel to the coast. I just managed to get into the headlight beam of the first car, waving my arms for them to stop. The first car slewed round past me, until its headlights again shone right on me, and stopped. Two men sprang out and challenged me in Italian, one covering me with a rifle, and I heard the click of the bolt. I shouted in Arabic, 'Salaam alaykum' (Peace be unto you), the same greeting the Lord Jesus used, and is the current greeting used today in Arabic and in Hebrew (Shalom alaykhem).

I heard a familiar voice say in English, 'Oh! My teacher, my teacher.' Sheik Musa Ga'as came running up to me and embraced me very warmly. I briefly outlined our predicament and asked if he would change batteries with us, if the voltage was the same. However, he would not hear of it. I pressed him to come into 'Edd and see if the sick woman could be taken into Assab or Massawa for medical help. This was too much, 'What! For a woman? Certainly not!' Islam gives a very low place to women in the order of things; they are expendable. He wanted to be on his way and to be in Thio before the sun became too intense. He said that he would leave word at Thio, and when the next Government boat came, it would radio news of us to Assab. In three days he would be coming back and would take some of us with him to Assab.

I reacted very strongly and told him that he must come and see this very sick woman and decide what could be done for her. I was sure that it was the Lord who had enabled me to intercept them. In desperation he said, 'Look, here is the very best medicine. Take this!' He gave me a bottle from his kit, which I could see contained Oral Penicillin tablets, total five million units. This was something quite new; I had not heard that there was such a form of Penicillin. I accepted it with thanks but I still insisted that he come into 'Edd. Eventually he reluctantly assented.

Dawn was just breaking as we drove into the village. Everyone was asleep on their string beds in the open, but began drowsily to get up at the sound of the cars. They had a tremendous surprise at seeing me dismounting with Sheik Musa, knowing that I had gone to sleep in the village the night before. Sheik Musa did not stay very long, he just saw a few of the village leaders. Before he left he shook hands with the elders, then came over to me, giving me a very warm handshake. It seemed amazing to them that the big Chief of all southern Danakil should be such a good friend of mine. His parting word was that he would see me in a few days time and take me with him to Assab.

I told Ibrahim how many tablets to give his wife, and when. I was certain that the Lord had provided them in a most remarkable way and that he knew his business.

Quite a stream of village notables came over to talk with me, no doubt because they felt that I was a good friend of Sheik Musa. However, the Lord was teaching me that in this warfare with Satan, such remissions of pressure, through help or patronage of earthly rulers or authorities, is very transitory. The only sure help and shield is the Lord himself.

The Lord prepares me for the battles ahead

Two days later, as I was having my Quiet Time, I knew that I had to open at the Psalms. I opened my Bible and was very conscious that my eyes were directed to some verses that I had previously coloured: 'Be still and know that I am God: I will be exalted among the heathen, I will be exalted in the earth' (46:10); 'The Lord of Hosts is with us; the God of Jacob is our refuge' (46:11); 'He shall subdue the people under us, and the nations under our feet' (47:3);

'He shall choose our inheritance for us, the excellency of Jacob whom he loved' (47:4); 'God reigneth over the heathen' (47:8); 'For this God is our God for ever and ever: he will be our guide even unto death' (48:14).

I knew that the Lord was speaking to me, but at the time I did not know what the immediate significance was. It did bring home to me though, that the Lord is sovereign *everywhere*, including Danakil.

Ibrahim wanted me to see his wife. This was the first time that I felt free to examine her. Her feet and legs were very swollen, as were her face and arms to a lesser extent. When I pressed her foot, a deep impression remained, showing that the tissues were waterlogged. I realized that the salt had been very bad for her. Her pulse was 120/min. and fairly strong, which made me think that it may not be the heart, but perhaps the blood. I examined her eyes and tongue. They were both deathly white; she was terribly anaemic. Ibrahim said that she had had a high fever before the penicillin, but now, two days later, I was sure her temperature was near to normal. I wondered how she could have lost so much blood and asked if she had had any severe bleeding. 'No!' said Ibrahim, 'That is trouble, the blood has not come away.' Apparently his other wife had had a very severe haemorrhage when she had her baby. He imagined that it should have been the same with this wife. I said, 'Dear Ibrahim, if this lady lost even a few drops more blood, she would be dead.' I asked about hook worm, blood in the stools and dysentery, but received no clues.

Then I asked how long she had been sick. She had been very healthy and strong until about seven months before. Then she had started with fevers and shivering and had steadily got worse, becoming weaker and weaker. I asked if the fevers occurred every day or not; it turned out that they were on alternate days. Then I understood; her red cells had been massively destroyed by malaria. 'Were there many mosquitoes about then?' 'Oh yes! They seemed to concentrate in the huts, and although it was the cool season, we had to sleep outside.'

I was thinking of getting the doctor in Assab to send some anti-malarial medicine when we got back, and thought I had better confirm the diagnosis by checking for an enlarged spleen. I asked Ibrahim if I may feel for her spleen, and he agreed. However, the abdomen was so distended that it was impossible to locate the spleen at all. I could not see that penicillin could be of help with malaria, but just then the Lord flooded me with understanding, and my heart was just overflowing with praise to him! The malaria was over, but had left her desperately anaemic and weak. Consequently, in that condition, the child was still-born. Also, having no resistance and in such insanitary conditions for her confinement, she had succumbed to deadly puerperal fever; a septic infection of the womb. She had been heading for certain death, and my own limited knowledge and understanding had been hastening the process, giving her salt which would aggravate the oedema. *But God had heard and answered prayer*, sending in a very wonderful way the *only* medicine, apart from the less effective sulpha drugs, that could destroy the germs and save her life. It was in a form that she could take. There was nobody within 100 to 150 miles who could have given her penicillin by injection, and oral penicillin was something very new; they did not have it in Aden.

Some very severe spiritual battles ensued, but it was a tremendous encouragement and joy to have Ibrahim coming day by day to tell me that his wife was picking up in strength and the swelling was going down.

Haj Yasseen had not come all day, the atmosphere had recently been quite tense. Muslim custom obliges them to entertain strangers, but to a limit of three days. This dear man had been providing for the five of our group for six days, and the only connection we had with him was that his son had had a lift in the lorry from Assab to 'Edd.

Spiritual Warfare for Danakil

I was sitting on my own in the shade, reading the Bible, when little Mohammed Othman came and asked what I was reading. I told him that it was God's Word, the Bible. 'Is it a good book?' 'Oh yes, a *very* good book!' Other children gathered around as little Mohammed asked me to read something from it. I started to translate the story of the Prodigal Son into Arabic.

Just then, the spiritual storm started to break. Little Abdul Ghaleb, Haj Yasseen's grandson, came running to us, scattering them all and fighting little Mohammed. He was shouting to them, 'Get away from him, he is a bad man. Do not listen to that book, it is a bad book. Get away, get away!' I was really dumbfounded, then the scandalous talk really started. Esa came over with it, and I heard him telling the others. The Nebi (prophet) had known that I had been to see Ibrahim's wife and was very angry indeed, especially at my touching her abdomen. I was completely blackened and under his curse. I gathered that the poor woman had to be taken down to the beach and dipped into the sea to purify her from her defilement. The evil and scandalous talk continued unabated; it was really an onslaught of hell. By Esa, I was called a dog, Satan and other things, and they all joined in. I just thought that if I did not have the Lord, it would seem like the end of life.

I began to think that our chances of getting into Danakil were doomed. Instead of using my name when referring to me, they used indirect names – such as Mr. Assab; the one who knows Aden, Assab, and 'Edd; Mr. Aden; or the one who knows Bellabuwee – in a way that everyone understood. Other names were Mr. Minus and the Dog of God. The scandal, the filth and the mocking just seemed to destroy me.

It was late evening and I was lying on my bed in the open, feeling really downcast and wretched. Then it came back to me what the Lord had showed me in his Word that morning: 'Be still and know that I am God.' 'I will be exalted among the heathen.' 'God reigneth over the heathen.' Such a lovely peace and assurance came over me and I knew that the Lord

Jesus was drawing me into his victory over all the evil and the powers of darkness. I began to understand in a much deeper way and to enter into the reality of the experience of Matthew 5:11-12: 'Blessed are ye when men shall say all manner of evil against you, falsely, for my sake ... Great is your reward in heaven... for so persecuted they the prophets which were before you.' I realized that in going forth with the gospel, I was entering into the same confrontation with the power of Satan that the Lord Jesus himself endured, as have done those who followed him ever since. Contrary to being defeated, I began to understand that we are more than conquerors through him that loved us and died to redeem us. Very quickly I was off into a wonderfully restful sleep.

The next morning, Sunday, my Quiet Time reading was 1 Peter 2:12, 15, 19-23, and 3:9-18. These were edifying and confirmatory words in the deep lessons that the Lord was having me learn experientially. He was feeding me spiritually. Following these and further trials, I was to be taken into the reality of God's sovereignty over the heathen and to rejoice in his deliverances.

After breakfast everyone was rather silent and sullen. I felt that they were rather ashamed of all the abuse they had poured out. Then Haj Yasseen came with a pan of hot water for me to attend to his foot. I heard him say that they wanted peace with me, as they did not want trouble with Sheik Musa Ga'as. He was very friendly and gracious to me.

That evening Lieutenant Abdullah told me that we had been invited to supper to the Quardhy (Religious

Judge) of 'Edd, Sheikh Khalifah Ali. They had a very big meal prepared and the Quardhy was very gracious. He was well educated and had travelled in Lebanon, Iraq and Iran, so he was interested to hear of our trip through the Middle East on our way out to Aden. After supper the Quardhy left and Sheikh Mohammed, the Quardhy's son, served us tea; he sat on the floor and attended to all the chores, while we sat on chairs. We walked back to Yasseen's compound in a very friendly spirit after an interesting and enjoyable evening.

The powers of darkness were by no means through with their attacks. In the early hours of the morning there was a really dreadful storm. Rain came in a terrific deluge, with little remission. For about three hours there was flashing of lightning and crashing of thunder, almost incessantly. The palm leaf matting roofs of the huts offered some protection against light rain of a short duration, but with this downpour it was just like a sieve. I tried to hold a sheet over me like a canopy, but the heavy rain came through that too and I was soaked to the skin. It became really cold, my teeth were chattering, and sleep was impossible. I was covered with wet sand which was washed off the roof matting. At dawn, everyone was clearing up and trying to get dried out, but in a very sullen and disgruntled manner. I saw Ibrahim and asked him to make sure that his wife was covered with blankets and kept warm.

The sorcerer

After breakfast they were talking about the sorcerer. Apparently it was very difficult for anyone to get to see him. If they were granted an interview, they were allowed not more than five minutes. They first had to put $E50 into a pouch in his belt. While they did this, he would raise his arms; at no time would he touch the money himself. When he heard their troubles or requests, he would tell them of something that would happen in the future, or warn them, or give advice. Also, if he agreed, he would put a curse on someone for them. They affirmed that when he put a curse on someone, dreadful things did indeed begin to happen to the person. I recognized this as Satanic power. He seemed to know all that was going on, partly through his servant, Abdu Rahman, and also I was sure, supernaturally, through Satan. Others got some news of him from his servant, for a few dollars a time. If Abdu went for food or any other necessities, he would take some money from the 'Nebi's' belt and also put the change back there. He very rarely left his house, and at times fasted from food and water. Everyone was in awe of him.

After all this talk, Lieutenant Abdullah and Esa decided to go over to Abdu Rahman to try to get some information. They returned with the news that the 'Oracle' was: 'The 'Nebi' was still furious with me over the matter of Ibrahim's wife. The dreadful storm was part of the curse, because of my presence in 'Edd and because I had touched the abdomen of Ibrahim's wife.'

The spiritual storm and the evil talk then recommenced as furiously as before. However, the Lord lifted me above it. One and another were coming to me for help. Ibrahim came with his wife's brother, and they were most grateful. The lady was improving rapidly and the swellings were going down. Haj Yasseen came and asked me how many days we had been with him. Indeed this was the sixth day. I asked what I could do to repay him or what I could send to him when I returned to Assab. At first he said, 'Nothing! Don't be ashamed,' but then he said that clothes or cloth would be acceptable. I was relieved that the matter was settled.

After supper the slander against me continued, led by Esa, referring to me as 'Abu (father) Assab, Abu Aden, Minus Seven'. The Lieutenant joined in, but I was very disappointed when Tewaldy joined in this time. I just ate my supper quietly, had a Quiet Time, and went to sleep, in the midst of all the evil and scandalous talk.

The next morning, Ibrahim came to say that his wife was improving rapidly and all the swellings were continuing to go down as I had told him they would. After Ibrahim left, the Lieutenant came into the hut. I greeted him and then he apologized for the bad talk. My heart just melted, and I said, 'I understand!' He said that it was because he was upset by all the difficulties and just having to wait. This opened up the way for a good heart to heart talk. I told him that we are in God's School, and one important lesson we have to learn is 'patience'. How could we learn patience without being made to wait? I told him how God wants to save us from sin, and to prepare us for and take us into his purposes. If we look to men, we are up and down. But when we come to know that God is true and faithful, then every day and every hour we can have his peace in our hearts, as we look to him and trust him. He said, 'This is 'Ta'am' (savoury food).'

Esa put his head in the door and greeted me rather sullenly. He said that he had been to see Abdu Rahman and was informed that the sorcerer had said that 'I was all right today; he had been angry with me yesterday, but not today'. I was not a bit enthused by Satan's tactic. The children and I had a happy time together and I was able to write down quite a number of Danakil words.

The next morning, I greeted Thompson and Esa in a friendly way. The Lieutenant was not at all in a good mood; when I greeted him he just scowled. During breakfast and after, he and Mohammed Fadhal carried on their coarse jesting at my expense, but I just sat on my bed reading the Word. Mohammed said, 'What sort of man is this? He doesn't flare up in anger, he is like a small child.' What a compliment! If only he had known it! ('Except ye became as little children...')

In the evening, when we put the beds outside, they were talking together. Thompson sat on my bed with me and seemed very friendly. However, he started to speak against the District Officer, Sheik Musa Ga'as. 'Look! He promised to come back in three days, and now it is the ninth day and he hasn't come. He doesn't care about us, nor does he keep his promises.' He went on to say that the coloured man on this side of Africa, when he gets into power, thinks that he is a king and only thinks of himself. He said that with the English people it was different, as it was with coloured people in Gold Coast; they could have authority without it going to their heads. He seemed quite sincere, and our conversation was in English.

I pointed out that the Bible had had a big influence in Britain and no doubt in Gold Coast as well. Jesus had shown us that true leadership was to serve, and to rule by love. I said that the Emperor Haile Selassie was loved by his people because they knew that he sought to serve them. However, Britain was becoming very godless, and was living on spiritual capital, and that the country was rapidly going down the drain.

The Lieutenant caught these last words and turning to the others said, 'He is saying that this country is going down the drain.' Immediately, the storm broke; even Tewaldy joined in, calling me all sorts of names. I just had to sit there and take it.

Thompson went over and joined them, and they asked him what I had said. He admitted that I had not said that Eritrea was going down the drain. But what he said was much worse; he told them that I had said that Sheik Musa was a Kaffir (nigger), that he was too high and mighty, and that black men could not rule. The devil was using damnable lies to seek to block the Lord's saving work in Danakil, and to destroy me, his servant by his grace. Then, what anger! What venom! Only the Lord knows all the slander and abuse that was poured on me. Thompson thought it a great joke. What a ghastly mess Satan can make of a person's character! However, the Lord's peace garrisoned me and I was soon asleep. Praise the Lord!

The next morning (Thursday 22nd July), after my Quiet Time, as the others awakened I greeted them.

They were very surly and the Lieutenant seemed quite unapproachable. I was left alone, but after some time Thompson came to the door and greeted me. I just said rather brokenly, 'Are you happy, Mr. Thompson?' He just passed it off and went on to speak disparagingly of Sheik Musa, saying that he had no thought of others, because he had not returned as he promised. I just turned away, picked up my prayer note book, and went over to the upturned boat on the beach for a time with the Lord for the rest of the morning.

When I returned, there was a remarkable change of attitude with the others. In the light of this, I felt sure that the Lieutenant, with his policeman's mind, must have doubted that Thompson had been telling the truth. He must have sent Thompson over to me, while they were on the other side of the palm leaf matting wall of the hut, testing my reaction as he spoke against Musa. My response had confirmed that Thompson's accusations had been a complete fabrication. The fact is, there was a complete change of attitude all round.

Around midday Haj Yasseen came for me to dress his foot. I said, 'I do want to thank you for all your kindness to me, dear Haj Yasseen,' and he just patted me on the knee in a friendly manner. I went back to the beach, continuing in prayer until I was called for lunch. At lunch the Lieutenant was quite different and we had a very good talk together on spiritual things. Again I returned to the beach for prayer, crying out to the Lord for deliverance, and the means for getting back to Assab. The Lord then gave me the assurance that deliverance was at hand.

I went back to the hut, just as Ibrahim came with the lovely news that his wife was very much better and that all the swellings in her arms, face, legs and abdomen had gone, and that she was feeling so much better in herself. He took me over to see the shark nets that he made.[1]

Over tea everyone was very kind, although a little unpleasant talk did enter in. Also, I heard Esa say that he knew very well that I was not from God; if God had been with me he would have done something because of all the time I had spent praying that day. *Little did he know that the Lord was about to make him eat those words.*

---

1. Nearly two years later, I heard from a shark hunter in Thio, that Ibrahim's wife, who had been so sick, was in good health and had had a baby boy. I also heard from Lionel some time later that he had visited 'Edd, and had met Ibrahim, who seemed to have really come to know the Lord Jesus Christ as his Saviour. The Lord really reached into that household in saving power, and I could certainly say, 'Of myself, I can do nothing.'

In September 1991, in comparing notes with Dr. Enid Parker, who has been working many years with the Danakil, I heard a further sequel to this. Enid has had very good help in compiling an Afar (Danakil) dictionary from Saleh, who is from 'Edd, and was then about 35 years old. Before he was born his mother had been so sick they had begun the funeral rites for her, but someone had been able to get some medicine for her that had saved her life. His mother's name was Khadijah, and she always received the missionaries very warmly. Some are convinced that she died a believer. Strangely she died of being allergic to Penicillin. It seems she knew about this and informed the doctor, but he possibly had not understood. The name of the father, that Enid remembers, was different, but it all points to the same family.

10

Deliverance

I went back to the beach to continue in prayer. It was just getting dusk when I saw a ship in the distance, heading towards 'Edd. My heart leapt with joy and praise to the Lord and I started to run towards the village. Some children, who were fishing, saw me running and then saw the ship coming in. They also ran towards the village, shouting out the news. Soon the whole village was out. What excitement! It was the *Sabeto*. It soon anchored about one and a half miles out.

The Lieutenant, Thompson and Esa went out in a Huri (native type heavy canoe), together with some of the Danakil fisherman, taking the battery with them. Later, I heard that the Huri had nearly capsized, both on the way out and back. They were away about two hours and the news seemed to be good. They had a new charged battery from the Sabeto, and had had our own battery charged up, but only for two hours. They had also been in radio contact with Assab and learned that after a week a Jeep had been sent to search for us. It had gone 180 kilometres without finding us. When there had been no news in two weeks, they concluded that we had perished.

It was arranged that we set off at 6 am the next day. If we did not reach Assab by late evening, a Jeep, with a battery and dynamo, would come to meet us. Everyone was very happy. However, Satan had by no means finished.

The next morning (Friday 23rd July), we were up at 5 am, packing and getting ready for leaving. We fitted the old battery back to the lorry, but it just would not start. However, it started on the new battery by hand cranking. Before we left I made sure of filling my canteen with sweet 'Edd water. We then had a lovely send off.

The first part of the journey went very well, and we arrived at Wadi. They filled a canvas bag with the brownish water from the water hole, for the radiator. The air was like that from a biscuit oven.

About thirty kilometres from Wadi, the engine started to misfire and, after a short while, stopped. I was parched with thirst; then, to my horror, I found that my water canteen was empty; the others had evidently drunk it all. The only water left was that in the canvas bag. I drank a good draft of it, and oh! it really was sweet, Guinea Worms or not!

We changed to the old battery. Probably with the engine being hot, it crank-started fairly easily, so we all jumped in again. We travelled another five kilometres before it coughed and spluttered to a jerky halt. With the new battery rested, it managed to take us another two kilometres. We were still about fifteen kilometres from Beilul, with no shade, and everyone was suffering badly from the heat, sun and thirst. The Lieutenant staggered past me and said, 'We're finished!' I responded, 'Lieutenant, the Lord has not let us down. When the battery first failed we just managed to get to 'Edd, where all our needs were met. Then, when we were giving up hope, the *Sabeto* arrived most unexpectedly. You will see that the Lord will not let us down now.' 'I hope you are right! I hope you are right!' he replied wearily.

Thompson was taking the caps off the old battery. He cursed and said that not only had they not charged the old battery, but they had not even put distilled water in it. I looked and certainly the tops of the plates were dry.

I knew that the Lord was showing me that we had to put water into that spent battery. I did not understand at the time how it could help. I told the Lieutenant that we had to put water in the battery from the drum. Thompson objected, especially when I poured some out of the nearly empty drum into an aluminium beaker which was rusty and reeked of kerosene. He said that if we put that water in, the battery would be ruined. The Lieutenant supported him. They only assented when I told them straight that if we did not do so, *we* would be ruined.

We then connected the battery to the terminals and cranked the engine. Wonder of wonders, the engine started with a healthy roar, so we all jumped in and off we went, making good speed, without the engine showing any sign of distress. We were all in a pretty bad state due to heat exhaustion and thirst. Although we were making good speed, there was still a grim apprehension. Yet we did go for about twelve kilometres before the engine began to misfire. The vehicle was going slower and slower, but it managed to complete the final three kilometres. It crawled into Beilul in the same way as we had crawled into 'Edd.

We all staggered out of the lorry and lay exhausted under the shade of palm trees on the outskirts of the village. The local people were very kind, bringing earthenware jars of water for us to drink as well as splashing water on us to cool and revive us. When we recovered sufficiently, we were escorted to various huts as guests of the village. It was only then that my mind began to work, and it dawned on me why the spent battery had shown evidence of charging after putting the water in. While the dynamo had been working, the water in the battery had also been evaporating, leaving charged plate above the lowered acid level. When the dynamo had stopped charging, only the part of the plate below the acid level was discharging. When we had put in the dirty water, this brought the acid level higher and in contact with plates that had some charge in them, enough anyway to take us the crucial fifteen kilometres. I was deeply grateful that my beloved Lord pressed me to do the right thing, even though I did not understand why at the time.

We had tea, then a meal, and I had a good wash and a shave. Sheik Abdullah was not there but everyone treated us very well. I was asked to go and see Esa's uncle who had a very swollen arm, tight with pus. I told him that it was a broken Guinea Worm, which was decaying inside. I advised him to go to Assab and have it lanced by the doctor who would remove the Guinea Worm.

In the same house was a boy, about ten years old, who was very sick. He was also very anaemic and had had fevers every other day for about twenty days; it was obviously malaria. The local medicine man had prescribed a native 'cure' – two rows of deep vertical cuts, with a sharp knife, around his waist, about ¾" long and about 1" apart. I recommended that Esa get some anti-malarial medicine from the doctor in Assab and send it back for him.

We were all rudely awakened at 4 am by a violent thunderstorm and torrential rain. Fortunately, the Beilul hut roofs were very thickly thatched with palm leaf, so only a few drops entered. By daylight the rain had stopped. Thompson came and asked if I would fit the new dynamo and battery to the lorry. It was then I learned that the police jeep had arrived at 1 am, driven by a police sergeant, bringing the dynamo and battery. When I had fitted them, the starter worked well, but the engine would not start. The sergeant tried towing it with the jeep, but the chain kept jumping off. He had only gone about fifty yards when there was another terrific downpour of rain. Everyone, including the Lieutenant, policemen, women passengers and myself, with the exception of Thompson and the sergeant, were absolutely drenched. After another hundred yards of towing, the truck was well and truly stuck in soft wet sand. They had to send back to the village for people to come and help push it, but even when they came, it would not go.

The Lieutenant then got really angry with Thompson, who replied that it was because I was with them that they had had all the troubles we had had. He gave Thompson a terrific verbal lashing. He said, in a voice like a whip cracking, 'Thompson, if you don't get this truck going in three minutes, YOU'RE THROUGH!' Thompson winced, tore around to the truck bonnet, dived his head down into the engine, tore back to the cab, tried the self starter, and the engine roared into life. He said, rather weakly, that the ignition had altered.

I realized that the Lieutenant had suspected that Thompson had deliberately altered something so that the engine would not start. He had got me to replace the dynamo and battery so as to have the satisfaction of being able to put the blame on me for the engine not starting. Certainly, when the Lieutenant rounded on him, he knew exactly where to go to put it right, i.e., to unscrew the distributor band and reset the timing. Instead of it coming on my head, it had come well and truly on his own head.

The Lieutenant came to me and said, 'Mr. Bevan, please come in the jeep with me.'

Some miles further on, the track wound down to a lava bed, to what had been the beach on our outward journey. The beach was not visible, but two hundred yards ahead, the track could be seen rising out of the water, over another lava bed. Inland, what had been a large desert area, surrounded by hills, was now a vast lake, and its waters were pouring out to sea, over what had been a two hundred yards stretch of beach, between the lava beds. The Lieutenant ordered the truck to try to cross. It rolled forward and down into the swift current. The water came over the axles and the exhaust was under water. We watched anxiously as it trundled across.

When we saw it mounting the other side the Lieutenant ordered the jeep to follow. I had to quickly pick up my attache case and a few other things, as the water swirled into the cab around our feet. We could feel the enormous weight of water pressing on our right side and dragging us seaward. The Lieutenant said grimly, 'I am beginning to doubt that we will ever get back to Assab alive.' It was only our forward motion and steering somewhat to the right that kept us from being washed out to sea. If water had got into the engine and it had stopped, that certainly would have happened.

It was with profound relief when the jeep began to emerge from the flood on to the lava bed. We then made good speed and began to think that it would not be long before we got to Assab. Just then we came over the brow of a hill towards what had been a dry wadi on our way out; now it was a deep river a hundred yards across. I went down into the water to test its depth; it came to my hips and was practically the same depth right across. It was quite impassible for the vehicles, so we would have to wait until the water level dropped sufficiently. We could see from the waterline on the banks that it had been falling. However, from inland, we could hear a dull booming sound as if a large waterfall was disgorging huge volumes of water into the wadi.

It was not till 6 pm that it was low enough to cross. The lorry went down the steep bank into the water and made its way across, its wheels riding up over big boulders. When it began rising out of the water onto the bank, there were loud cheers. The Lieutenant ordered the jeep to cross. It went down the steep bank, but became stuck with its nose down in the water and could go neither forward nor backward. All the men then tugged, pushed and removed boulders, and eventually got it moving. It went forward, mounting boulders, until half-way across it mounted a big boulder with an awful grind. It was leaning at a crazy angle, with the left-hand wheels spinning in the air. We had a terrible job heaving and straining, but eventually we managed to get it off. Two of us then went ahead, clearing boulders to make a path for the jeep to cross. There was a deep sigh of relief when it was on the far bank. That was the last obstacle we encountered, and we arrived in Assab about 8 pm.

Everything was covered with thick dust in the SIM Mission house. I had left some things in the fridge and was able to have a meal. It was so hot that I only had on a pair of shorts. I was going through the dark sittingroom to the veranda to sleep, when I leapt into the air with a cry of pain. It was as if my foot had been pierced with a red hot needle. In agonizing pain I hopped over to the switch to turn on the light. I was very surprised at not finding anything that would account for the terrible pain in my right instep. I must have walked near the junction of two carpets. When I lifted one up, there, scampering away, was a large black scorpion which I quickly dispatched.

I had seen people writhing in agony for hours, with beads of perspiration standing out on their foreheads, because of a scorpion sting, and only relaxing when the doctor injected local anaesthetic at the site of the sting. Later, they would begin to tense up again, as the effect wore off.

With this in mind, I knelt by my bed and laid it before the Lord, while writhing in terrible pain. I told him that I was worn out and desperately in need of sleep, putting it all in his dear hands. I remember crawling into bed, but nothing more until waking the next morning. There was just a faint tingling in my foot, after having had a very refreshing sleep. My heart was just full of praise and thanksgiving to my beloved, faithful Lord Jesus.

During the next few days I wrote to Lionel and to others who were interceding for us. One to whom I wrote was Miss Hollie Welch, who was leader of the WEC missionary prayer battery of which I had been a member. I told about the deliverance from the effects of the scorpion venom, and about having drunk water possibly infected with Guinea Worm. I quoted Mark 16:18: 'They shall take up serpents; and if they drink any deadly thing it shall not hurt them.' A few weeks later I received a reply from Hollie. She wrote that during the time I was stranded in Danakil, the Lord was getting her up two or three times in the early hours of each morning, especially to pray for me. She had a consciousness that I was being assailed by the powers of darkness. In her letter she wrote, 'I will give you a better verse, Bevan – Luke 10:19.' 'Behold! I give you power to tread on serpents, *and scorpions*, and over all the power of the enemy ...'.

The next day I went to see the Italian doctor at the little hospital. I told him of every case I had dealt with in Danakil. He was delighted and said that he would send medicines for each case, and ask Sheik Musa to despatch them to where they were needed.

There was a letter waiting for me from Dr. Bernard Walker from Tiberias in Israel. In it he wrote, 'I seem to remember that your call from the Lord was to Israel. If you believe it is of the Lord, the door is open for you to come and work with us in the hospital in Tiberias.'

I was overjoyed at the faithfulness of the Lord, and how he had shown me, in taking me to Aden, that it would be his school for me and *his door for me to Israel.*

Sheik Musa Ga'as Returns

I heard that Sheik Musa had returned the previous evening, and that one of his jeeps had broken down in Thio.

The next day I went to the District Office. There were many waiting in the large hall to see Sheik Musa, as he had been away for nearly two weeks. After a while he came out of his office and was just greeting one or two when he caught sight of me. He came towards me with outstretched hands. He took my hands in his and said, 'Oh! Mr. Woodhead, you have had many troubles. I warned you not to go, you look so very thin and weak.' 'But strong in spirit and praising the Lord, Sheik Musa,' I replied. 'Look!' he said, 'I arrived in 'Edd a few days after you left and I heard of some of the things that happened. The people need you. I have strongly recommended that they receive you and they are waiting for you.' I felt full to the brim with gratitude to the Lord, and embraced Sheik Musa.

Back at the house I just wept. Satan had thrown in everything and had done his utmost to discredit me and prevent us from getting into Danakil. The Lord had graciously overruled. He had even turned it into our door of acceptance from the hearts of the people and also from their Chief Administrator.

The next day I wrote to Lionel, then in the USA, telling him of the trip up country and also of Dr. Walker's invitation to Israel. I also wrote to Elsa Gundersen and Marion who was with her on holiday at the time, letting them know the news and suggested that we get together with Jack and Kath for a Field Council Meeting to seek the Lord's will for the next steps. I asked them to get a plane to Aden, stopping off at Assab from the 18th to 20th of August, and I too would go to Aden.

I had given Lieutenant Abdullah a gift of money to be divided among Thompson, Esa and Tewaldy in gratitude for letting me share in the trip. I saw him on the Friday and he said that they all appreciated the gift. I then went to buy cloth, bandages and other useful items for Haj Yasseento to cover the cost of my stay in 'Edd, and packed them up with some gifts for others. I included a number of Arabic Bibles and New Testaments for Haj Yasseen, the Quardhy (Judge) and others, as I had promised. All this was to go up, with the medicines, on the next Government boat.

I was conscious of the Holy Spirit pressing me about making sure the gifts, Bibles and medicines were dispatched, and that the Lord was showing me that it was important for his purposes. I kept enquiring about the Government boat. On Monday 9th August, I heard that the *Sabeto* had arrived, so I went to see Sheik Musa about the medicines. He assured me that the medicines would be dispatched on the boat, so I was glad that the matter was in hand.

Then I went to the harbour with the box for Haj Yasseen.[1] The customs let it through without charge, and the captain of the boat would not charge me.

On Wednesday 18th August 1954, I went to meet Elsa and Marion when they arrived by plane. Back at the SIM house, during and after lunch, we had a good time sharing all the news. They were thrilled at the way the Lord was manifestly opening up Danakil to us.

The next day we went to see Sheik Musa Ga'as and he was extremely friendly. He asked if we could open a clinic in 'Edd and one in the Buri peninsular which is the northern limit of Dankalia, just south of Massawa.

That afternoon, we went to see Ato Chanlau. When I told him that Sheik Musa had asked us to open clinics in 'Edd and in Buri, he was delighted and said, 'Oh! This is wonderful, do you think you can do something for Aussa?' Aussa is the Ethiopian part of Danakil.

That afternoon Bud and Dot Acord arrived back on a plane that was reportedly cancelled. It was lovely to see them back and they seemed just bubbling over with love and joy. Bud said that he too was going to Aden. He and I went together by boat.

---

1. Some years later, I had a letter from Lionel saying that he had been in 'Edd and had been with Haj Yasseen a few days before his death. When Lionel had been speaking of our salvation through Christ and his atoning death, some of the men disputed with Lionel, but Haj Yasseen told them to be quiet and listen, as all that Dr. Gurney was telling them was the truth. Lionel was sure that the dear old man had truly come to faith in Jesus.

11

Return to Aden

We berthed in Aden on Monday, 23rd August 1954. Jack and Kath had made such a lovely home for the Team that it did really feel a homecoming to be with them once again.

Elsa and Marion, of course, were already there. For the next three days we had informal field council meetings. Elsa started with a review of the Ethiopian situation. We discussed the doors the Lord was opening to the Danakil. Also, how to proceed if the Lord opened up the way for me to go to Israel.

The following day, Marion said she had had a very wonderful, clear word from the Lord from Haggai 1:4-8, especially verse 8. She said that the Lord had applied it to her personally: 'Is it time for you, O ye, to dwell in your ceiled houses, and this house lie waste .... go up .... and build the house.'

The following day, we closed our discussions with a very precious time of prayer. Marion seemed full of joy in the Holy Spirit. Although she came in for a time of severe satanic attack, she was used later in pioneering the work for the gospel in Danakil and afterwards in Yemen.

At the meeting, I met George Morris, a new Church of Scotland doctor working at the hospital at Sheik Othman. I was immediately drawn to him and to his dear wife, Margaret, a doctor and a surgeon like her husband. They were very prayerfully interested in the opening up of a work in Danakil.

The following day we saw Elsa off to Addis, from Aden airport.

Lionel, and my call to Israel

I received a letter back from Lionel on 12th September. He had not had any leading from the Lord, but said an emphatic 'No!' for me to go to Israel. He said that he was away from the field and the Lord was obviously and very wonderfully using me in getting the opening into Danakil. If I left at this stage, I would be letting him down badly.

I was really concerned to know the Lord's will. Jack and I agreed together to ask the Lord for a definite seal. If the Lord wanted me to go to Israel without undue delay, we asked that within four weeks from that day, he would provide the money to cover my passage to Israel. If not, I would take it that the Lord wanted me to stay for the Danakil openings. I wrote about this to Lionel.

As the month went by, I felt that it was not a test of faith, in which case the Lord may leave giving the answer until right at the end of the month. It was rather to know his will, either way. So when the 10th October passed, and the seal of the passage money had not been given, I had the full assurance that the Lord wanted me to stay for the opening of Danakil.

I then wrote to Dr. Walker about the Lord's leading and said I was still sure the Lord wanted me in Israel, but it was clear that the time was not yet. How he would open the door in the future I did not know, but it was in his hands.

The Lord then clearly confirmed that the leading was from himself. On 15th October, I had a letter from Elsa telling me that the Eritrean approval of my resident's visa had arrived at the immigration department of the Foreign Office in Addis Ababa (although it was nearly nine months before I finally received it). Then through different channels came various gifts and tokens that were just needed for opening up work in Danakil.

The first was a 2cc syringe from one of the Danish missionaries. Then Sister Bobbie Bain of the Keith Falconer Hospital, who was retiring after many years service, gave us a good deal of needed household equipment. This included a pressure cooker which we later found very useful. Within a few days, there was a valuable gift of medicines and medical equipment through the Maxtons of the Sudan Interior Mission in Ma'ala, Aden. There were gifts of money from various sources. Also, a package of Scripture portions arrived from the Scripture Gift Mission. They were in a number of languages used in Eritrea – Tigrinia, Amharic, Arabic, Italian – and I do not know who had asked them to be sent to me. It became so clear that the Lord was with us, supplying the things that would be needed for the entrance of the gospel into Danakil.

Marion had gladly registered her willingness to pioneer the entrance into Danakil. The Scottish Hospital badly needed Marion's services, and she had promised them six months, from September onwards. However, towards the end of September, she was very sick and had much pain. She was hospitalized, treated and declared fit for service anywhere in the tropics. Towards the end of October, she was again feeling and looking very ill. It was confirmed that she had amoebic hepatitis. The Church of Scotland folk not only agreed but insisted that she be invalided home and a passage was quickly arranged for her. It was nearly a year before she was well enough to return to the Field.

Some medical training

At the beginning of September, Dr. and Mrs. Morris invited me to supper. They were eager to hear all about Danakil. Of special interest to them was how the Lord had used a cheap first aid kit and some very scanty medical knowledge in 'Edd. I asked if it would be possible for me to get some medical training and experience at the hospital. George was very enthusiastic and said that by all means he would do what he could to help.

He had a tremendous job on his hands without an extra burden of giving me training. He had an eighty-bed hospital to care for, operations two days a week, and outpatients of approximately fifty people another two days a week, plus visits to other patients in the town. Margaret was part-time looking after the home and part-time helping in the hospital. This included women and children's outpatients of about seventy patients twice a week, and quite often taking part in operations. In addition they were trying to learn Arabic. Nevertheless, George and Margaret spared no effort to give me all the training they could.

I was with George practically the whole time.

While sitting with him in his outpatients clinics, he would make comments on nearly all the cases and explain instructive cases in detail. It was the same when on the hospital rounds and in the theatre; he gave me as much as I could absorb on diagnosis and treatment. Almost every day I had lunch with them, after which George instructed me on the various aspects of medicine such as the vascular system and the nervous system. He loaned me medical books to study and then would question me on them. I was encouraged to apply what I was learning to cases he would give me to examine. He would point out signs and symptoms I had missed. I was shown the results of laboratory tests and he would ask me to give the diagnosis and suggest the therapy. Eventually he had me scrubbing up and assisting in operations. This involved catching bleeding arteries, handing the surgeon the instruments, and suturing up while he scrubbed up for the next case. He also saw that I got good practice in giving injections, lumber punctures, spinal anaesthetics and draining plural effusions.

Bruno and Peter arrive
On November 29th 1954, two new members arrived to join us on the field. Bruno Herm was from Germany and Peter Dahlen (pronounced Darleen) was from Australia. As I mentioned earlier, Bruno and his brother Daniel had been students at Beattenberg Bible College in Switzerland where he Lord had used Lionel in leading both of them to have a call to the Moslem world. Bruno was led to join our Team and Daniel to join Jack Ringer in the Afghan Border Crusade. After

Bible School Bruno trained for one year at the Missionary School of Medicine in London.

Peter's father had been a Swedish Consul in Australia. Peter came to London with a scholarship to study journalism at University. He came to know the Lord through a London City Missionary, Tom Gray, who later became the Team's Home Secretary. Peter's spiritual experience completely altered the course of his life. His only desire was to serve the Lord. He had some male nursing training, and also worked for some years with the Scripture Gift Mission. In addition he completed a Wycliffe Linguistics course. Both Peter and Bruno had been highly recommended as those who loved the Lord Jesus and were keen soul winners.

They both got down to studying Arabic, taking lessons with Rev. James Ritchie in Sheikh Othman. Also they were, particularly Peter, sitting with Arabs in the market and eating with them in the eating houses. They were picking up Arabic idiom and expressions, and above all getting to know, understand and love the people. Bruno was concentrating on the Boys Club, so to be able to take over when Jack was on furlough. Peter concentrated on colportage and personal contacts, although Bruno took part in this also.

Each day when I came back from the hospital, Jack, Kath, Bruno and Peter would be interested to hear what interesting cases we had had and what operations we had done. On one occasion, after some operations, we went over to Dr. Ahmed Affara's house for refreshments. Selwa, his younger daughter, said,

'Uncle Bev, my dolly is broken. Could you please mend it for me?' It was a movable head sleeping doll, and the head was off. I asked if I could have a piece of stiff wire, some elastic, and some plaster of paris. These were provided, and I succeeded in replacing the head so that it could move as before. Naturally, Selwa was delighted. Later, back at Bait Ashereef, they asked what operations we had had. I went through the list and, managing to keep a serious face, said, 'Oh yes! We had to graft on a head.' It was great fun to see the look of astonishment on their faces, changing to incredulity, and then an explanation being demanded.

The battle for sufficient sleep

We did have fun, and good laughs together, although there was always a sense of spiritual battle. Satan used many devices to oppress and depress, to get us down physically and spiritually. He had many ways of preventing us from getting proper and sufficient sleep. It was a battle to maintain our Quiet Times. Every morning about 4 am the powerful loudspeakers of the mosques would blare out calls to prayer. Very often we were prevented from getting to sleep at night.

Opposite Bait Ashereef there was a favourite place to hold a Mokhtera, which is held in a huge temporary structure. A man wishing to marry invites many guests to his Mokhtera, money is collected from them, and they are served soft drinks, cigarettes and qart. There would be blaring music each evening until the early hours of the following morning – and each Mokhtera lasted a week. If his profit was not enough to buy the

137

bride, he would hold a few more at intervals.

Another means the enemy used to deprive us of proper sleep was an invasion of bugs. Many of the men and boys in Aden had no homes. They used what was known as the '20 cent Hotel'. All along the streets, men hired out beds made of wooden frames and having a palm leaf string mesh. These were hung up on the street walls on hooks during the day. At night they were taken down and the streets were lined with sleeping men. Looking down on to the street in the morning, we could see the 'hotel' keeper slapping the bed strings with his sandal. As bugs fell to the ground, he would despatch them with his big toe.

I suppose a number of the boys who came to the club slept out on these beds. Well, the bug invasion came to the flat, which was above the club. We all started getting big, red irritable lumps on various parts of our anatomy, and our sleep was very disturbed. We couldn't find anything for sometime and didn't even realize that they were bug bites. Once we found some bugs, then there was no doubt. We tried many things to get rid of them, but to no avail. We enquired about the habits of bugs and this led Bruno to putting the legs of his bed in tins containing kerosene. He found that this made a big difference. This gave us the key to effectively deal with the problem. We mixed gammexene with water and painted it all around the bottom of the legs of the beds, chairs and tables, making sure that no part of the bed or bedding touched the wall. In this way the bugs had to walk over the gammexene when going to and returning from their victims. This did the trick. After about a week the battle was won, and how thankful we were.

Later, the Lord used this knowledge and experience as one of the ways we were able to help the Danakil, when we established our first station in Thio. The Lord used our trial, and victory, as a blessing to others, and the furtherance of his purposes.

My engagement to Elna

In April 1946, through Rev. Ricard Madsen, Elna Andersen had experienced God's call for her to go to Aden. She applied to The Danish Missionary Society, having heard of a vacancy for a teacher in the Danish Mission School in Aden. However, they wanted one who could weave to run the Weaving School when Karen Olsen was on furlough. As Elna had only one hand, the right, they concluded that she could not cope with weaving. But she was sure that God wanted her in Aden, so she went to a weaving teacher to be tested. After a few hours at weaving and other kinds of handwork, the teacher gave her a recommendation which satisfied the mission and she was accepted.

They sent her to a weaving school for five months. Eventually she was weaving her own dress lengths and tablecloths, as well as designing patterns, setting up looms, and all manner of handiwork.

Since she would have to learn Arabic through English, she was sent to London to study and get practice in English. After London, she was to go to Beirut for nine months Arabic study. At that time there was a senior missionary from Lebanon doing deputation work in Denmark, Miss Anna Jacobsen. Because she was travelling around, Elna had not succeeded in contacting her by the time she had to leave. She caught the midnight train at Fredericia. When she entered her sleeping compartment, she saw that there was a white haired lady asleep and saw from a luggage label that it was Anna Jacobsen. The next day they had good fellowship together and were delighted to find they were both travelling to Genoa. They had further pleasant surprises when they found they were sailing on the same boat and given the same cabin. How wonderfully thoughtful and kind is the Lord. Those who wholly trust him are especially privileged to experience, and recognize, this.

Elna stayed at the British Syrian Mission while studying Arabic. Her teacher was sister-in-law to Esa Haddad, with whom Lionel and I had had such lovely fellowship in Basra. Esa had taught Elna for a few days while he was on holiday with his wife in Beirut, because Elna's teacher was sick. When he learned that Elna was going to Aden, he asked her to give his warm love to Dr. Gurney and his friend.

When we first met after she arrived in Aden she had these greetings to give me from Esa. Some time later I realized that our hearts were being drawn together, although we did not correspond when I went across to Ethiopia and Eritrea. On returning to Aden I was waiting on the Lord for his will concerning our deepening mutual regard. I was getting clear leading that it was from the Lord.

Through dear Karen Olsen we were able to meet on 12th January 1955, and really face all the implications together, and open our hearts to one another on all the issues. I told Elna that I had given my life wholly to the Lord, and although I believed he was calling me to Israel, I was his servant to go wherever and whenever he would send me. I had no salary and looked entirely to him to supply my needs, according to his promise. I was only free to ask her to marry me if she could accept those terms. She replied that that was all she wanted. She also had sought the Lord, and had had clear guidance that it was indeed of him.

I had not told Elna that I only had enough money to last about two weeks if I lived very stringently. Sure enough the money was almost gone after two weeks. I thought then, 'Seek ye first the kingdom of God and his righteousness, and all these things shall be added unto you.' If our relationship was not of him it was very easy for him to show it by withholding my support. In which case, to be true to the Lord, I would have to ask Elna to release me from our engagement. Just at that point a letter arrived from Gypsie Perkins telling me that she had received an anonymous gift for me of £25, and I would know what it was for. If I wanted the money right away, I could draw that amount from the mission account, and let her know. Elna was really delighted when I told her.

It was precious to get such hearty congratulations from our missionary colleagues, mission leaders, including Elna's Home Board, and friends. Miss Mette Skovhus, one of the veteran Teachers from the School, was home in Denmark at the time. Although the School would be losing a teacher, she visited Elna's parents and put in a good word for me. Elna's parents told her that whoever Elna chose was right in their eyes, so there was a warm welcome awaiting us in Denmark.

Lionel recognized that it was of the Lord, and after a meeting of the Team Council, Elna was given a warm invitation to be a member of the Team following our marriage. We agreed to leave the wedding for eighteen months to give The Danish Missionary Society time to get a replacement for Elna.

The birth of the indigenous church in Aden

The words Lionel had spoken in Beirut when he heard that Marouf was going to Aden were indeed prophetic: 'Bev, I believe that God is purposing to build his church in Aden and he is sending Marouf to be a pillar.'

In the various missions over the years there had been one or two converts in any given period. Sometimes they were standing their ground and living in victory. At other times fear was stifling their witness and they would be rather joyless and defeated, but still believing. Some turned back to Islam.

In the spring of 1955 there were one or two converts in each of the missions, attending the Sunday Arabic services in the churches of the respective missions. Most of those attending were Muslims, and the sermons were invariably the gospel message, which those who believed had already accepted. When the words 'Son of God' were spoken, some would spit, get up and walk out, and maybe throw stones inside. There were some weekly Bible studies, but mostly of unbelievers, but no real fellowship and building up in faith, which the few believers needed.

Peter Dahlen seemed to have this as a real heart burden. At times it would come from his heart like a voice crying in the wilderness, *The believers ought to come together*. On Tuesday 17th May 1955, Marouf was visiting us in Bait Ashereef, and with Bruno, Peter and myself, we were talking about various topics. This cry again came from Peter's heart, '*The believers ought to come together.*' It just dawned on me, a revelation, what that cry meant in relation to the handful of believers. I said to Marouf, 'Do you understand what Peter has just said? The believers are attending these formal services in a passive way, hearing the gospel over and over again, which they have already accepted, in the presence of Muslims. They have no real Christian fellowship, and only a little building up in the Word. Why don't you gather these believers together, and let us missionaries keep out? Have a time of fellowship together, around the Word, with the Lord in the midst.'

Marouf slapped his thigh and said, 'I believe that is it!' We said we would ask the missions if they would agree. We committed it to the Lord, and agreed to hold on in prayer. We would try to arrange the first meeting in Bait Ashereef, in the flat above the club, the following Sunday.

The missions agreed, and seven (a very significant number) were gathered together at 8.15 pm in the 'Upper room' on Sunday 29th May 1955. It 'happened' to be Whit Sunday (Pentecost) in the providence of God. Praise the Lord! It was like a spiritual atomic bomb, bringing together a critical mass of atomic potential. The converts were overjoyed; they had a lovely time of testimony, prayer, getting down to the Word, and real fellowship. The Lord was manifestly in the midst. They said that it was wonderful to be in the company of fellow Arabs, and to tell what the Lord had done for them, and be greeted with great joy, and praise to the Lord, rather than spitting and abuse.

They were all given power to witness boldly. Despite fierce reactions their numbers grew, until by the time we left Aden in July 1956, there were seventeen believers in the Fellowship. Sometime later we heard that it had grown to twenty-seven. However, severe persecution followed. When news of the meetings spread, and the time and place became known, angry crowds would gather around Bait Ashereef. The believers had to have police protection to make it possible for them to get to the meeting. A number of them were thrown out of their jobs, and others threatened. The heart of one failed him for fear. In order to get back in favour with the Muslims, he went about the streets around Bait Ashereef shouting, 'They are deceivers, Mohammed is the prophet, and the Koran is the book.'

When the believers heard of it, Marouf gathered them for three days of prayer and fasting, pleading for him before the Lord. After some days he came back, broken in repentance and sorrow for betraying the Lord Jesus. He could not see how the Lord could possibly forgive him, nor how the believers could forgive him.

In a small but vital way, Marouf, together with his dear wife Suad, was like a Moses bringing the believers through a wilderness of testing. They were sheltering some and feeding them in their home, and helping them in their trials in other ways. It must have been deeply grieving to the Lord when the enemy succeeded in tearing the infant church apart into two groups. This was over the issue of infant baptism or the baptism of believers by immersion. Whilst there was very good understanding and cooperation amongst the missionaries on the field, they had their own conviction on such matters. However, the Mission Boards of the Church of Scotland and the Danish Mission could not have had the same feeling of tragedy, in insisting on the form the infant church should take. After all they had had their missions in Aden for many years, and some of the original converts were fruit of their outreach.

Marouf felt deeply that there should be freedom of conscience and conviction for the individual believers. Although the Red Sea Team was interdenominational, and had members from churches with differing views on baptism, they felt that they should stand with Marouf. There was a good spirit between the two groups, and they would attend each other's special functions, such as baptism.

Just before the original seven believers had their memorable meeting, through colportage work Bruno and Peter came into contact with Mohammed Beihani. Beihani used to sit in the Fish Market and seemed to be a person of character. Those who sat around had a great respect for his opinions. At one time he had had some knowledge of the Old Testament through a Jewish friend, and often longed to have a Bible for himself. He asked Bruno and Peter if they could get an Arabic Bible for him, and they did so. He was in the grip of qart, and at first he had great difficulty in breaking the habit. Although he believed that the Bible is God's Word, it took some time for him to let go of the idea that he could earn his own salvation. It also took time for him to realize that, although repentance is vital, we can only be reconciled to God by faith in Christ and his atoning work on the cross.

Later, Beihani was appointed pastor of the group following infant baptism. However, all were to have their baptism of fire, and fear, when a Communist regime took over and the missionaries were forced to leave. God was doing a refining work. The silver, gold and precious stones will be refined, and the wood, hay and stubble will be burned up. *Every man's work shall be tried with fire to see what sort it is.* May he use his refined and tested servants to bring his light and love to Islamic darkness. This is a challenge to all of us to bear them up in prayer.

There were what seemed to me long frustrating delays in getting my residence visa for Eritrea. After eight months delay the visa came through in June 1955, but then I was told that I could not go until I had an entry visa. This arrived on 5th July. There were several boats a week going to Eritrea, yet it was two weeks before I could get a passage. Peter Dahlen was to accompany me across and then return to Aden on the same boat.

What followed showed that the Lord's timing was perfect.

12

The Lord Opens the Door to the Danakil

We arrived at Assab on Friday, 22nd July, 1955. The next morning, I went to see Ato Chanlau, the Chief Secretary. He greeted me very warmly and then quite overwhelmed me with the following words: 'Mr. Woodhead, *God has sent you on just the right day.* Today is the Emperor's birthday. Tonight, a reception will be held in his honour at the Government House. Many Danakil dignitaries who are presently in town will be there. The guest of honour is Sheikh Yassein Mahmoud, Amir of Thio. You are invited, and I will introduce you to Sheikh Yassein, and ask him to help you get your mission established in Danakil.' On hearing that Peter was with me, he kindly extended the invitation to include him.

He told me that Sheikh Yassein was a very important man in Danakil. He had been one of the Eritrean delegates present at the United Nations conference, when the future of the country had been decided. The UN resolution was to hold a plebiscite, which resulted in the majority voting for Eritrea to be federated to Ethiopia, thereby ending the British Mandate. Within this capacity, Yassein had visited the USA, and also to Italy and France. Ato Chanlau informed me that Sheikh Yassein would be sailing to Thio on the *Silee*, which was due to leave for Massawa on the Monday afternoon. If I was organized, I could pass through customs on Monday morning, and sail on the same passage. Without doubt, the Lord's timing was wonderful. My heart effervesced with praise and wonder. Back at the boat, Peter and I joined to express our gratitude to the Lord.

That evening, Ato Chanlau introduced me to a number of the Amhara officials and Danakil dignitaries, including the Quardhy of 'Edd, to whom I had already sent an Arabic Bible. Then we were introduced to Sheikh Yassein. He was astonishingly affable and sociable, and I spent about a third of the evening conversing with him. He suggested that, as we would both be sailing on the *Silee*, we would be able to talk further. Later, Ato Chanlau manifested his delight that I had got on so well with Sheikh Yassein. The next morning, Peter left to return to Aden.

On the Monday, I cleared my luggage through customs, and boarded the *Silee*. My first priority was to seek out Sheikh Alameen, the new District Officer of southern Danakil. He had been appointed in place of Sheikh Musa Ga'as, who had been promoted to Senior District Officer. This meant that the entire coastal region of Eritrea which was exclusively Muslim now fell within his remit.

Sheikh Alameen seemed sincerely glad to meet me and appeared to approve of our projects for the Danakil. However, he stressed that we would have to take the people's feelings into consideration. It became clear, later, that he meant we must not attempt to change their religion.

Ato Chanlau had instructed me to collect a letter of recommendation intended for the Asmara authorities. He showed me the letter addressed to Ato Samuel, Director General at the Interior Ministry, which stated that I was a 'known friend' – which meant that I had been vetted and approved. This letter was later to be a decisive factor in the authorization of our mission.

The *Silee* did not leave until Wednesday noon. That afternoon, evening and the next morning were spent in conversation with Sheikh Yassein. The first topic of discussion was the Danakil language. He displayed genuine interest in my notes and glossary. It was the first time that he had read anything in his own language.

The conversation then turned to spiritual matters. Suddenly, impressed upon my mind was a comprehensive and graphic outline of what I had to say to him. This was something novel to me, yet I knew deep in my heart that this was what he should hear from me. It constituted to all intents and purposes a frontal attack on Islam and, humanly speaking, it seemed definitely the wrong approach. It flew in the face of a piece of wise counsel that Lionel had imparted to me, 'Bev! You don't have to fight darkness to get it out of a room. You simply let the light in, and the darkness is dispelled.'

Nevertheless, I ventured, 'Sheikh Yassein, have you ever read the Bible?' He admitted that he had not. 'Well, I have read the Bible many times, and I have also read a substantial portion of the Koran. Both claim to be of divine origin. They have much in common, but some assertions contradict each other outright. It follows, therefore, that they cannot both be of God. I am absolutely sure that the Bible is the Word of God, and that the Koran is not.' At this he became irate and retorted, 'Prove it!' I replied that some tenets of the Koran have a ring of truth, but in fact are false. This suggestion stoked his anger further. 'Tell me one such case, and prove it,' he challenged.

Taking up the gauntlet, I said that the Koran depicts God's Judgment as being by 'Mizan' ('balance'): a man's good deeds are put on one side of the scale and his evil deeds on the other; if the good outweighs the bad he goes to heaven, and if the bad outweighs the good he goes to hell. 'Well! That is right,' he rejoined. I replied, 'It seems fair, but it does not represent justice. "Equity", as it is portrayed in the Koran, does not correspond to God's weights and scales.' Again he barked, 'Prove it!'

I set forth the example that had so clearly come to my mind: 'A certain man is hard working, extremely conscientious, and most considerate and caring toward his family. Moreover, he has donated over $E1,000 to the poor. Would you consider him to be a good man?' 'Of course,' he replied. I continued, 'But supposing that he got into financial difficulties, and accumulated debts of $E300, which he was subsequently unable to repay. So he decides to break into the shop of a rich merchant, who, so he figures, would barely miss the money. He manages to steal $E500, to cover his debt, allowing $E200 for himself. He's fairly confident that he will not be found out. Let us suppose that the police discover incriminating evidence against him and, using trained hounds, track him down. On trial, the case against him is proven, forcing him to admit his guilt. However, the counsel for the defence point out that his record at work and at home was impeccable and that he had donated over $E1,000 to poor people. His only crime was to have stolen $E500. Would the Judge weigh his good deeds against his evil deed, and say, "The good outweighs the bad. You are free"?'

Sheikh Yassein gasped as he realized the absurdity of the notion. He himself was a judge.

I said, 'The judge would surely identify his good deeds as the fulfilment of his duty and the theft as a crime and, therefore, liable to punishment. Furthermore,' I added, 'God's standard of justice is absolute and unbending. Regardless of what good Adam had done previously, he was rightly condemned for his sin. That one act of transgression was punishable by expulsion from the Garden of Eden and, ultimately, by death.'

Sheikh Yassein smote his thigh and declared, 'You people have got something that my people need. I am going to help you get your mission established in Thio. You must open a school too. I will send my children there, and encourage many others to come. He then informed me that he planned to take the next boat to Asmara and, once there, would escort me into the highest halls of office and request that permits be issued. He sincerely wished to help and happily accepted an Arabic Bible. Our stop-off in Thio lasted just half an hour, but within that short space of time he introduced me to both the Deputy District Officer and the police lieutenant.

Situated in the Doldrums, Massawa was, as always, oppressively hot. Nevertheless, whilst in the city, I took the opportunity to visit Sheikh Musa Ga'as, who, on account of his promotion, had moved to Massawa. He greeted me very warmly, and reaffirmed his friendship and support, saying, 'We are your friends.' He told me that once our permission was granted, if we wanted to start in Thio, he would give me a letter of recommendation to pass on to his brother, Ahmed Ga'as, who was chief of the market in Thio. If we wished to start in 'Edd, his cousin was sheikh of 'Edd, and he would provide me with a letter to give to him. The next day I took the bus to Asmara.

Once in Asmara, I headed for the Paradiso, the SIM missionary rest home. The Emmels immediately made me feel welcome. On Tuesday, I was able to see Ato Samuel at the Interior Ministry, and pass on Ato Chanlau's letter declaring me a known friend. He was eager to help and, in no time, I was supplied with a resident's visa and identity card.

It was six weeks before Sheikh Yassein came to Asmara. In the meanwhile, I read up on the Federal Act, and the Constitution of Eritrea, only drawn up recently. I discovered that the freedom to teach and propagate any religion was guaranteed therein. Under the Federal Act, the Ethiopian Government had overall responsibility for government through the Emperor's Representative (in this case Betawadad, the Emperor's son-in-law, husband to Princess Tenanee Worg – herself a sincere believer). He directly controlled the Foreign and Interior Ministries, as well as Customs and Excise. The Eritrean Federal Government, comprising locally elected ministers, retained a certain amount of autonomy, insofar as they are responsible for Health, Education, and Social Services.

This meant that our mission and individual residents' visas ultimately had to be approved by the Emperor's Representative. In addition, our medical work and school initiatives had to be passed by the Eritrean Federal Authorities. The senior ministry, apparently endued with supervisory powers, was the Ministry of Social Services.

I drafted an application and the Emmels approved it. A copy was sent to Lionel, whose suggestions for amendments were then incorporated into the final draft.

Sheikh Yassein arrives in Asmara

At regular intervals I enquired at Pensione Augustus whether Sheikh Yassein had arrived. On Thursday, 8th September 1955 I found him present. He gave me a hearty welcome and said that he had tested the climate in Thio and the local folk were favourable to our coming. The acting District Officer of Thio, whom I had met on the boat at Thio, had expressed pleasure at the prospect of our arrival. Sheikh Yassein was now calling me by my first name, Bevan, and even took my hand as we went out into the town. Our first stop was the palace grounds, where Betawadad's office was located. In the corridor Sheikh Yassein spotted a man to whom by-passers were bowing. Yassein ran over to him. They embraced and talked a while. Afterward, Yassein explained that it was the newly elected chief executive of the Eritrean Federal Government.

He said that the most efficient method of obtaining permits is to by-pass the usual channels and go straight to the top. We arranged to meet at the palace on Tuesday morning, when Yassein promised to introduce me to Ato Hailu, the Chief of the Cabinet. He was the one who arranged all Betawadad's appointments, and practically the only one who had unrestricted access to Betawadad. Ato Hailu said that he would speak to His Excellency, and inform me of the proposed appointment by phone. I assured Sheikh Yassein that I would let him know as soon as I had heard. Ato Hailu rang the next evening, and announced that His Excellency would see me at 10 am the following day.

On Thursday, 15th September, I rang Sheikh Yassein who said that he had a business engagement, but would try to be at the palace for 10 am. However, he had not arrived by the time I was ushered into the presence of the Emperor's Representative. He was very courteous, and we conducted a brief conversation in English, after which he sent for his interpreter. I outlined our aims and plans. He said that if we worked in the spirit indicated, and not as some other missionaries who meddled in politics, he would be most happy to help us. He described Ethiopia as an island of Christianity. He said that it was very difficult to convert Muslims to Christianity. We must therefore target the young people and set up schools. He stipulated, however, that the Amharic language be part of the school curriculum, as a shared common language constituted an essential element of the unification of Ethiopia – a goal which they pursued. I objected that should our nurses be required first to learn Amharic, our projects would be greatly delayed. He pointed out that that would not be necessary; we need only recruit an ex-mission boy, a Christian, who spoke Amharic and Arabic. He would teach them. I conceded that we could probably manage that. Having agreed to submit a written application, I returned his warm handshake and took my leave of him. The entire meeting had lasted an hour.

On 29th September, I handed our application to Ato Hailu, who promised to pass it on to His Excellency. It detailed requests for a Headquarters in Asmara, a forwarding base in Massawa, and mission stations (quantity unspecified) in Danikal. In addition, application was made for ten residence visas, one for each team member, the names of which I listed, and one for each missionary candidate. As it transpired, it was fortunate that I had specified the number, as the authorities were less interested in the names of the applicants, than in the quantity of visas required,

Ato Hailu undertook to arrange a translation of the application for official use. On 18th October he contacted me again to inform me that His Excellency had left for Addis Ababa, where he would seek an official approval of our application from the Ethiopian Government.

Ato Mubrahto Berhay, Director of Medical Services
In a letter arriving 26th September 1955, Lionel made a suggestion which proved to be of vital importance.

It led me to a key figure, who was of great assistance in hastening our final approval by the Federal Eritrean Government. Lionel had asked me to enquire if we could obtain medical supplies through the Government Central Medical Stores. I approached the civil hospital's administrator the very same day. He explained that it was not within his capacity to decide such a matter, but rang up Ato Mubrahto, the director of medical services for the entire country and arranged an interview for me there and then.

I was ushered into his presence, feeling somewhat embarrassed as I was wearing my oldest clothes. Some high officials construe this to be a sign of disrespect in such circumstances. I apologized for my appearance stating that I had no idea that I was to have the privilege of meeting him face to face. He understood, and smiled in such a way as to put me at ease. When I explained the purpose of my interview, he replied that there were other missions in the country doing medical work. There was no arrangement for them to obtain supplies through the Government Stores. However, if there were some items we could not get elsewhere, he would consider giving permission in such cases. He asked about the nature of our mission, as he had not heard of it before. He said that our application for the medical work would automatically pass through his hands, so it would be best if I gave him a copy, and he would be able to look into it. He explained that it would speed up matters when the time came for him to deal with it officially.

Then I mentioned that I had received some field medical training and wondered whether any opportunities were open to me to gain further training while awaiting our permits. He emitted an enthusiastic 'Yes!', instructing me to submit a written application and assuring me that he would endeavour to help.

I handed Ato Mubrahto the two applications the next day and went to see him again later. He told me that Dr. Tassi, the Italian medical director of the one thousand-bed hospital, had agreed to give me instruction and practical experience in the various departments. I would then sit an examination, and, if successful, would be awarded a certificate enabling me to work as a medical assistant.

When I knocked on Dr. Tassi's door, I found him expecting me. Our conversation was constructive: he outlined in brief the direction my training would take. To start with I would be under the direct supervision of the heads of various departments for several weeks at a time.

When I actually came to start, Dr. Tassi instructed my superiors in turn to maximize my training and practical experience, stressing that we would eventually be benefiting the Danakil.

In all, I covered several wards: medical, surgical, ear nose throat, gynaecology and obstetrics, finishing in the large eye hospital. I was also given the opportunity to carry out various tests, such as on urine and blood, in the pathological and serological laboratories, and was even transferred for a period to the pharmacy. A solid friendship formed between myself and Dr. Labate, the serologist. He would show me specimens that he had collected in his private laboratory. Sometimes he would switch to English, in order to improve his knowledge of the language. Other times he would discourse on medical matters, such as the nervous, digestive or vascular systems. Often he would invite me to his home for supper to share in the warm family environment.

Our application to the Eritrean Federal Government was handed to Ato Abraham, Deputy Director of Social Services, on 7th November, 1955. Copies of our application to the Health and Education Departments were also required. He would then see these departments, and also His Excellency, and the chief executive, personally, on our behalf.

Satan's Dividing Tactics

Understandably, as the Lord was graciously opening doors by means of high-ranking contacts, Satan was at work to disrupt. He was exploiting our human weaknesses, to sow dissension within the team. He is not ignorant of certain truths. Rather he uses his knowledge to serve his own evil ends: 'A house divided against itself cannot stand' (Matt. 12:25).

I was unaware how pride was taking root. I was attributing undue significance to 'my' Field, at the expense of the others. I reasoned that, as we had limited personnel and resources, we could not afford to expand in two Fields. It was necessary to concentrate on one. Of course, I considered 'my' Field to be of paramount importance. Jack's heart, by contrast, lay in Aden. He was keen to expand the work and set up team headquarters there. Only later did I realize that the problem resided in distorted vision: my gaze was fixed on 'our' rather than 'God's' resources.

Lionel had been away for over two years. His vision was enlarging from the Red Sea to encompass the whole Muslim world. I felt that being the only doctor his place was to spearhead the medical thrust into Danakil. I was unable to appreciate the vital part the Lord had assigned him in raising up a sizable army of prayer warriors. These were indispensable if Satan was to be defeated and the captives of Islam set free. Equally essential were the stewards, whose resources would be available where the Lord required them. The plight of multitudes of Muslims, prey to Satanic deceits, was being conveyed to young Christians far and wide. The challenge issued was for these youths to train as doctors and nurses in order to join the battle for souls. Indeed, many of these would respond, some ending up at our side.

Gypsie was by nature an orderly person and liked to have everything structured and regimented. This was an attribute, to a point. Satan, as I saw it, recognized this organizational flair to push her into a role of leadership. Gypsie began forming an advisory council from a body of mature Christian leaders. With the help of a Christian lawyer, she set about drafting a constitution which effectively gave her control over the Team from the home end. Word of these initiatives prompted voluminous and sustained correspondence on our part, as we sought to press home our views on the matter.

By God's grace we began to be deeply and prayerfully concerned about the entire issue. The Holy Spirit began pricking our consciences, highlighting attitudes that displeased him. He began opening our eyes to the value of each other's functions. He was gradually dissolving all trace of hostility and arrogance, drawing us to himself, reconciling and restoring our Team.

It struck me again just how much Christian work is run by human reasoning and expediency. The energy and natural ability of the flesh slowly but surely asserts itself, squeezing out the Holy Spirit, often thereby thwarting the Lord's specific purposes. This was the trap into which we were being led, the result being strife and confusion. Often apparently prosperous and impressive institutions are established. Yet as long as each one pursues his own concerns, such organizations serve only to spawn similar fruitless self-perpetuating bodies.

The Lord had put me in a very wonderful school, for which I am deeply grateful to him. I cherish the fellowship he gave me with his choice servants and all he taught me through them.

I received another letter from Dr. Bernard Walker on 15th October, 1955. He congratulated Elna and I on our engagement and reminded me that the door to Israel was still open. I asked the Lord whether I should construe this as a nudge on his part and, if so, to make it plain. Later, I turned to prepare the message I was to give the next day, Sunday. As I opened the Bible to find my place, I opened at Psalm 122, and my eye was directed to the second verse: '*Our* feet shall stand within thy gates ,O Jerusalem.' I understood the word 'our' to signify myself and Elna.

Marion's 'fleece'

Marion had since recovered from her amoebic dysentery and sailed at the end of September 1955 to Cairo, for six months or more Arabic language study.

On 3rd of December, I received a letter from Marion, saying that she felt the Lord was pressing her to go to Asmara. She had covenanted with the Lord that, if it was of him, he should grant her a resident's visa for Eritrea before Christmas. If it did not materialize, she would stay on in Cairo until the end of 1956. Well, that was a very tall order. Indeed, it would be nothing short of a miracle. We had no written permission as yet for our mission, and the application had only gone to Addis Ababa mid-October.

I committed it to the Lord and went to the palace. I found the spacious corridor packed with all kinds of people of many nationalities: important business people, diplomats and others. His Excellency had only just returned from Addis, after an absence of six weeks. It looked as if it would be weeks before I would have any chance of seeing him, and he was the only one who would be able to grant such a visa. I just stood in the corridor, and prayed, 'Heavenly Father, you who are the ruler over all principalities and powers. I just commit this to you, in the name of our Lord Jesus Christ.'

As it happened, I was standing outside the door of Ato Hailu's office. His door opened and, as he came out, he almost bumped into me. He greeted me with a friendly smile. I told him that the opportunity of recruiting a highly trained and experienced nurse had arisen, but I needed to obtain a resident's permit for her before Christmas. If I failed to do so we would have to wait another twelve months. I underlined that she would be a real asset to the medical team. I continued that our team leader, Dr. Gurney, was expected soon too, to open up the Danakil medical work, and we needed a resident's visa for him also. He explained that His Excellency was only just back after being away many weeks, and was extremely busy. However, he said he was just going in to see him, and he would put my case to him. Emerging from His Excellency's office, he handed me a note signed by Betawadad, and instructed me to make an appointment with Ato Qumulatchu, His Excellency's executive.

On Monday, 5th December, I was able to see Ato Qumulatchu. He asked if the permission for our mission had been granted. I replied that it was, at least, in principle.' He gave me a note for Ato Samuel, Director of the Ministry of Interior.

Ato Samuel disclosed that Ato Qumulatchu desired supplementary information. He asked about Dr. Gurney's sojourns in Ethiopia and I told him what I knew. He also asked about Marion. He did not seem satisfied and started looking through the papers in my file. He stopped at one letter and I recognized it as the one penned by Ato Chanlau. After reading it, he immediately rang up Ato Qumulatchu. Although he spoke in Amharic I could follow the gist of the conversation. He reported that Dr. Gurney had been expelled from Ethiopia and that he had given medical assistance to Ethiopian refugees in Somaliland. He told him about the letter from Ato Chanlau, describing me as a known friend, and affirmed that my visa had been approved in Addis Ababa. Ato Qumulatchu replied with few words and then the conversation was over. Ato Samuel turned to me, smiling, and said, 'Come this afternoon. I will have the residents' visas ready for you, for Dr. Gurney, and for Nurse Marion Thomas.' I told him about the seal that Marion had asked the Lord for, and the wonderful way in which God had answered. He was aware of the obstacles involved in obtaining a resident's visa, not least the tremendous delays. He was evidently touched.

Gypsie Perkins' Visit

On 24th December, I received a letter from Gypsie announcing that she had inherited a sum of money. This would pay for her trip out, enabling her to visit the fields. She planned to sail on 16th December, accompanied by two recruits, Nurse Agnes Crozier of Canada and Nurse Joan Mason of England, who would be following a language study course in Cairo in preparation for the Danakil field. After helping them find their feet in Cairo, Gypsie would then complete the final stage of her journey to Asmara together with Marion.

Lionel wrote asking me to get a post office box, with a number that could be easily remembered. Also, he asked me to look around for a suitable house to rent, which might serve as our headquarters. He said that it should be fairly near the centre of Asmara, yet quiet and secluded, if possible in its own grounds. It should not be too large or expensive, but capable of extension, allowing for the team to expand. The criteria Lionel gave me seemed too demanding, even unrealistic: near the centre but secluded; rented but capable of extension. However, as things turned out, I am sure the Lord had given Lionel a mental picture of the actual place he had chosen for us. The description and conditions corresponded so accurately with the one we soon found.

I did not have much choice with Post Office Box numbers but selected POB 226. After prolonged house-hunting, the only sensible options were out-of-town houses, with a monthly rent of about $E200, which seemed very expensive.

I arranged for Elsa to come to Asmara, as Gypsy and Marion were due to arrive on 26th January, 1956. I figured we could all stay in Paradiso.

When they came, I took them sightseeing and house-hunting in a garry, a horse-drawn carriage. Being a polio victim, Gypsie depended on a specially-designed walking-stick. Her distress was understandably great when she witnessed her stick fall and snap under the heavy garry wheel. I searched in vain for a replacement. As I had a rendezvous with Dr. Labatay, I mentioned the matter to him. He did not know of a supplier, but asked me to show him the stick. Together, we found a second-hand furniture shop that sold sticks. Alas, none were suitable for Gypsie. As we were there, I though I might at least ask about the furniture. I did so, explaining to the retailer that we were seeking a flat and would probably need furniture. He said he knew a lady who wanted to rent a flat, and offered to take us to see her.

It was simply amazing. The flat was a fair size, yet the proprietor was asking a mere E$80 per month. It was half of a big house in its own grounds and fully furnished. She said that in twelve months time we could rent both halves if we wished. It was very secluded, yet only ten minutes walk from the centre of Asmara. It was exactly as Lionel had specified, and truly a gift from the Lord.

I had a further rendezvous with Dr. Labatay. On meeting, he handed me Gypsie's stick, beautifully and professionally repaired with the joint carefully concealed by a silver band. '*He* does all things well,' he remarked simply. Naturally, Gypsie was overjoyed. Dr. Labatay refused any payment.

In the middle of lunch on Tuesday, 7th February, 1956, Lionel burst in on us, hardly able to contain his joy in the Lord.

Mr. Duff was at Paradiso and invited us all down to Ghinda, promising to take us to Massawa the following day. In Massawa, we visited Sheikh Musa Ga'as, and received a warm reception. We had heard that our application had not yet been passed by the Ministry of Social Services, as they were awaiting a reply from Sheikh Alameen. Sheikh Musa said that he had approved it and would send a telegram to Sheikh Alameen to petition him to hasten matters. He confirmed further that he would give us letters of recommendation addressed to the Sheiks in Thio and 'Edd, when we were ready to set up our stations.

The Duffs were going on furlough and asked if Marion could take over the work at Ghinda while they were away. We all felt happy with this arrangement, and thought that it would benefit Marion to spend time with the Duffs before they left.

Changes in Aden

Some Danish Mission council members had come out to Aden, and the question of infant baptism had been raised. This was possibly on account of the situation with the infant church, but the position of those assisting the Danish Mission, such as Jack, Bruno and Peter, came into question. The Danish Lutheran Church are not opposed to adult baptism, even by immersion, but strongly object to anyone being, as they say, re-baptized. A question mark was placed over the suitability of such persons holding responsible posts within the Danish Mission. Jack committed it to the Lord, accepting that if he could not help with the club in Aden, then the Lord was indicating that he wanted him in Asmara. Eventually, the Danish Mission decided that Jack and Peter were unsuitable, as they had been re-baptized. Bruno was permitted to continue in his post as he had only been baptized once, albeit by immersion as an adult believer. One council member was rather grieved at the apparent inconsistency in policy. 'We can accept Muslim lady teachers in our mission school,' she objected, 'but we cannot accept a brother in the Lord, because he has been baptized twice.'

Gypsie left for Aden on 9th February, and Elsa for Addis the following day. Before they left it was agreed that Jack and Kath should come to Asmara for one year. They should take over the running of the headquarters, which was to be a supply and support base for the advance into Danakil. Elsa was meanwhile to stay in Addis, as we were seeking the Lord for an entry into Ethiopian Danakil. Lionel and I moved into our very first Red Sea Mission team headquarters on 13th February, 1956.

Progress in Asmara

Lionel and I obtained an interview with His Excellency on 16th February, and Lionel conversed with him in Amharic. Betawadad said he had granted our application, and referred us to Qumulatchu for further related queries.

We had heard on 13th February that the permits had also been granted by the Director of Medical Services, Ato Mubrahto, and by the Director of Education, Dr. Matthews. We did not yet have a permit from the Director of Social Services. He was awaiting a response from Sheikh Alameen, the District Officer of Southern Danakil.

Jack came to Asmara on 12th March, while Kath was to join him later. He wasted no time in taking matters in hand: he was an excellent organizer, and, so it emerged, an excellent cook. The two boys, Raymond and Michael, had temporarily been placed in the care of the Missionary Children's School of the Bible College of Wales, in Swansea.

Marion came up from Ghinda on 24th March for a Field Council Meeting. This was to review events, to pray together, and to wait on the Lord for his leading, especially as regards the final permit. The hold-up lay with Sheikh Alameen, whose permission was tied up with the proviso that we renounce the intention to teach the gospel. The Ministry of Social Services had also withdrawn the permit for medical work.

At the same meeting, the invitation was officially extended to Elna to become a member of the Red Sea Mission Team. The membership would take effect as from our marriage, which was arranged for mid-July. I would be responsible for financing her fare home. My fare would be paid by the Team. Both our return journeys would be covered by the Team, provided we commit ourselves to a full term in the Field.

An answer to prayer: the final go-ahead

On 26th March, I went to see Ato Mubrahto. He had asked for a Bible-study aid, so I brought him Dr. Joe Church's book, *Everyman a Bible Student*, and told him that we had ordered a medical missionary book for him. He was very grateful and delighted to report that the objections that had been tabled, concerning our application, had been overruled. We were to be issued our permit at last. Clasping my hand in his, he added, 'Mr. Woodhead, British blood has been shed on the soil of Eritrea, and British bones have been buried here. We have a deep debt of gratitude to British people, and many high officials feel the same way. Anything I can do to help you, I will.' Later, Ato Qumulatchu likewise affirmed that we had full official permission to realize our projects.

Praise the Lord! The door to the Danakil had been opened.

Chapter 13

'He Opens and No Man Shuts'

Frank Eshelman, a school teacher in the prodigious American Army Camp in Asmara, and his wife, Marcine, took a very keen interest in our Team. On 26th March, Frank announced that he had just over a week's holiday, and Doc Wilson had offered to hire out his jeep to him. He had decided to go hunting into Danakil and asked if I would accompany him to act as an interpreter. Knowing we were hoping to open a station at Thio, he said he would endeavour to go that far. It was surely of the Lord. We left Wednesday, 28th March, 1956. In Massawa, we made a beeline for Sheikh Musa Ga'as' office, hoping to obtain the promised letters from him. To our deep disappointment we heard that he had gone down into Danakil, and probably on to Assab.

After camping overnight at the south end of the Gulf of Zula, we took the track in the direction of the Buri Peninsula. The path turned north, and eventually evanesced leaving us on a comparatively broad long ridge, running north. The sides were too steep to negotiate, and sometimes even precipitous. The whole surface was formed of volcanic boulders, with no trace of a road or track, and no alternative route in sight. It was extremely hard-going both for the jeep, and for poor Frank trying to manage the vehicle. We were advancing at a snail's pace and it was the shape of the boulders, which we had to hurdle one by one, that determined our course. Frank seemed to have minimal control. Within three hours we had covered about ten kilometres. Poor Frank was absolutely exhausted, so we decided to camp. I made a fire and after supper we had a time of prayer, not omitting to present to the Lord our pitiable circumstances.

I was up about 5.30 am, and came across two Danakil men herding their flock of goats. I greeted them in Arabic and asked for directions to Thio. They pointed north, signalled with their hands that we were to head east after a short stretch.

We realized that the Lord had indeed answered our prayers, so we were in much better spirits. After breakfast, we set off again, continuing north, then after about half an hour the ground levelled out and we discerned a track, which after a short while veered eastward. The going was then considerably easier, our path taking us across a plain, studded with acacia thorns. We reached the beach, running south, then the track crept a little inland, out of sight of the beach. We passed two coastal villages which, according to the map, were probably Bardoli and Mersa Fatma. It seemed that the next habitation was Thio, 90 km further south.

Me'ider – God's Perfect Timing

After about 70 km, we spotted some vehicle tracks which veered off left, towards the coast, and over the top of a sand dune we distinguished a minaret. We decided to turn off into the village to establish our bearings. At the entrance to the village stood a police hut. Enquiring there the identity of the village, we were informed that it was Me'ider; Thio lay some 20 km further south. I asked about Sheikh Musa Ga'as, and was told that he was in the village, together with Sheikh Alameen; the District Officer of Thio, Shaheem Gidar; the police lieutenant of Thio, Tilenty ('Lieutenant'); the Quardhy ('Religious Judge') of Thio; and other dignitaries. The officer then offered to take us to Sheikh Alameen. We were warmly received, and invited to some refreshments. After this we excused ourselves, and our guide took us to Musa Ga'as. Musa acknowledged our presence with unbridled enthusiasm. 'This is wonderful!' he exclaimed. 'All the officials whose approval you need to open your station in Thio are here.' Pointing to our guide he announced, 'This is my brother Ahmed Ga'as, Chief of the Market of Thio. He is one of those to whom I was intending to write a letter on your behalf.' Proclaiming us his guests he arranged for a hut to be provided for us and for all our needs to be met. He recommended that Ahmed Ga'as take us to Thio the following day, to introduce us to others there and suggested we make enquiries about accommodation with a view to establishing our mission.

The occasion of this gathering of Danakili leaders in Me'ider, was the official hand-over of the authority of Musa Ga'as to Alameen, as the newly installed District Officer of southern Danakil. He would remain subject to Musa Ga'as, recently appointed Senior District Officer for the whole of the Eritrean coastal territory, which included southern Dankalia. Our unintentional intrusion upon this important summit was quite evidently the Lord's doing, and we were once again filled with wonder and gratitude.

The next day, Ahmed accompanied us to Thio, where he took us to the police station and the Federal Government office, and to view some houses and huts. Despite some friendly faces, we were eyed with suspicion by the predominately aloof officials.

When we arrived back at Me'ider, preparations for a bright and colourful wedding were in progress. Frank and I were about to take some photographs, when a young man angrily forbade us. However, we were made guests of honour. They had heard that I had medicines with me, and I was whisked away to attend to a very sick man, Haj Abdu (Nakoodha). He was barely conscious and was running a dangerously high fever. All the signs pointed to malaria. I gave him some chloroquine, and said that I would return the next morning.

Back at the wedding there were festivities, tribal dances and the like. I think some of the dignitaries were a bit bored, and rather piqued by Frank's beautiful telescopic rifle and shotgun. They asked if we would take them hunting, so we went off in the jeep just as dusk was falling. As we were leaving the village, they spotted a jackal. Frank dropped it, first shot. These beasts play havoc with the chickens and young goats. We went over and they cut off its tail as a trophy, their eyes dancing with glee. A little later, Frank felled another jackal, again with a single shot, about 150 yards away. They repeated their ritual with even greater ravishment. About a quarter of an hour later, one of them pointed to a hyena, barely distinguishable in the dusk, loping along towards the village. It was a long shot, but again the first shot dropped it. Those with us were all leaders from Thio. They were almost wild with excitement when they cut off the animal's tail. Hyenas are very destructive; they bite great chunks from the rear of a camel or a cow, and often the victim has to be killed, as it would almost certainly die. The leaders were eager to regain the village, in order to put the trophies on display.

When the news spread, practically all in the village came to file past the trophies. I think this spectacle aroused far more excitement than the wedding, it meant such a lot to them. As for us, we were treated like heroes, deliverers.

The next morning, I went to see Haj Abdu. He was sitting up in bed, looking considerably livelier, but complained of a bad headache. His temperature had dropped from 103 F to 99 F, as had his pulse, measuring 75 as opposed to the previous 110. I gave him some more chloroquine, and some aspirins for his headache.

We heard that Musa Ga'as and Alameen had left in the early hours of the morning. In the afternoon, the village, assembled in a large hut, appeared to be holding a council meeting. We discerned sounds of a hubbub. Raised voices echoed from within. We could make out the words 'Americani', 'Ingleezi' (English), 'Hakeem' (doctor), and 'Mubashereen' (missionaries), and realized that we were the centrepiece of the angry debate.

Withdrawing to our hut, we got on our knees before our beloved, almighty, heavenly Father in the name of our Lord Jesus Christ and through his shed blood. We entreated him to grant us victory, and entrance into the land. Aware that the shouting in the distance had subsided, we stepped outside to see a substantial crowd moving in the direction of our hut. They appeared to be calm, even sympathetic. Indeed, their manner was by no means confrontational, rather, they sought medical assistance. Amongst them was the young man who had snapped at us when we had attempted to take photographs. It seemed he was suffering from a gastric ulcer. I told them that a qualified doctor and myself were hoping to open a practice in Thio, at which point we would have the appropriate medicine with which to treat them. They seemed relieved and grateful. Shaheem, Tilenty and Ahmed then approached, supporting a Muslim teacher, whose leg was crippled. Judging by his fanatic views, we guessed that he had instigated the opposition. They asked if we could design a special boot for him. He had broken his leg years before, and it had set by itself, causing a significant shortening of the limb. I measured the difference in length between the two legs, and said that we would do what we could to help him. His satisfaction was evident.

We went to see Haj Abdu, who had recovered remarkably. Both his fever and headaches had disappeared and his appetite was returning. He was so grateful and confided, 'All in Me'ider are glad you came, you can stay twenty years if you wish.'

We set off for Asmara just after noon, following a touching send-off. On the way, Frank shot a gazelle to take home. It was dusk as we were crossing Buri.

The going was easy till we hit upon the dreaded boulder ridge, subjecting us to another three-and-a-half-hour gruelling drive. Poor Frank was sick with disappointment to find that, with all the jolting, his shotgun had fallen off somewhere along the track. We camped for the night at 10.30 pm.

Back in Asmara

Lionel and Jack were deeply thankful to the Lord for bringing us back safely, and for giving us further encouraging signs that he was indeed opening the door to the Danakil for us as a team.

The next day, I went to Frank's home. The gazelle meat smelt obnoxiously. It was evidently not edible. With the loss of the gun, and no game, the trip was a fiasco as far as the hunting was concerned. However, the Lord seemed to have given dear Frank and Marcine a hunger for the high calling of God in Christ Jesus. I am sure the Lord was showing them that he had a specific purpose for their lives.

Lionel and I began to organize in earnest our move to Thio to start our first team mission station.

On Friday, 6th April, 1956, I introduced Jack to Ato Mubrahto and Dr. Verdacchi. When Ato Mubrahto understood that Jack would be staying on in Asmara, he asked if he would give him English lessons. Jack consented and they arranged to meet twice a week. Ato Mubrahto rejoiced with me over our impending trip.

He arranged for me to sit my exam on the 12th April. On the day, I discovered that four doctors would be examining me, including Dr. Verdacchi. The examination completed, they immediately announced that they would award me 95% of the marks. They appeared to be fully satisfied with my performance. Pending receipt of the official certificate, I was nevertheless permitted to practise as a male nurse.

On the 9th April, I was able to introduce Jack to Ato Qumulatchu. He received us warmly, and was most interested to hear of the trip to Thio. He declared that, with regard to our schools, Sheikh Alameen and the Social Affairs Ministry were quite out of order forbidding us to teach the gospel. Under the constitution, each individual reserves the right to practise and propagate his own religion.

He said that he would give me a letter which I was to pass on to Colonel Legassa, His Imperial Majesty's Representative in Assab. He was authorized to grant us permission to open schools and to teach the gospel in Dankalia. The said letter arrived promptly on the Saturday morning. All obstacles preventing our advance into the Danakil had been cleared by him, of whom it is said, 'He opens, and no man shuts, he shuts; and no man opens' (Rev. 3:7).

On hearing that Sheikh Yassein had been admitted to hospital in Asmara, Lionel and I went to pay him a visit. He was delighted that all the necessary permits had finally been granted, and that we had had been so eagerly received by the Danakil.

Jack did a fine job finalizing preparations for our trip to Thio. Many came to bid Lionel and myself farewell as we boarded late Wednesday evening.

Our first night was thus spent on the *Silee*. At dawn the next morning, Thursday 19th April, 1956, Lionel was at the bow of the ship, having his quiet time. Thio was visible in the distance, providing a picturesque backdrop. Sidling up on tiptoes, so as not to disturb Lionel, I snapped a few shots with my camera. I felt a lump in my throat as I recalled that twenty years before, the Lord had given him Genesis 28:15 as a personal promise: 'And behold I am with thee, and will keep thee in all the places which thou goest and I will bring thee again into this land...' Here, the Lord, wonderfully and faithfully, was fulfilling his promise before my very eyes.

We dropped anchor at 10 am, and were enthusiastically received by the villagers, especially the children. Some of them helped us carry the bulk of our belongings to shore in a rowing boat. The District Officer, Shaheem Gidar, arranged to have them stored in his office, as we had planned to visit Assab before settling in Thio. He and Sheikh Ahmed said they would have accommodation ready for us by the time we returned.

We rejoined the *Silee* which continued its course to Assab, arriving at 3 pm Friday. We spent the remainder of the afternoon visiting various friends. Saturday, we had an interview with Colonel Legassa, the Emperor's Representative in Assab. He was very gracious and happily accepted Ato Qumalatchu's letter. After reading it, he stated that, according to the Constitution, we were at liberty to teach the Bible in our schools. He advised us, nevertheless, for our own sakes, to be tactful with the local people and with the Eritrean Government. As far as he was concerned, we could open schools and clinics in Danakil, and teach the Bible.

We then visited Sheikh Alameen, who was as cordial and helpful as ever. He wrote a letter for us to take to the District Officer of Thio, in which he requested the use of a stone house for our accommodation and work purposes.

We arrived back in Thio on Tuesday, 24th April, 1956, and were again the object of a heart-warming welcome from the Danakil assembled on the quay. As they helped us unload our goods from the rowing boat, they cried, 'Ya Bevan! Where is Frank? Is this the doctor? Is he a real doctor?' Lionel just laughed, and I assured them that he was a genuine doctor.

At this point, it is as well to say something about Thio. It is a coral peninsula, measuring one and a half miles in length and between a quarter and a half a mile in width, and protruding into the sea, at right angles to the coast. The Danakil village extended from about half way from the coast to three quarters' way out. The furthermost quarter was the site of the former Italian headquarters, from where they exercised control over the Danakil territory. Among the few remaining buildings still intact was the former Italian Governor's palace, and a large single-story wooden building, once an Italian hospital, now converted into a school. In addition to these stood a garage, flanked on either side by a 16 ft. square room. The structure was of coral blocks, with a flat concrete-slab roof.

Thio certainly presented itself as the ideal location for our headquarters, for a number of reasons. Being a peninsula, it was fanned by a constant sea-breeze, regardless of the direction of the wind, creating a cooler climate during the day, but providing for warmer temperatures at night. Also, it was spared the dust-clouds which one could almost always see sweeping along the coast.

Near the tip, on the northern side, a stone harbour wall had been built out, like one side of an arrow head. This provided an ideal deep-water harbour for the Government boats to drop anchor, when they called in on their outward and homeward monthly trips, between Assab and Massawa.

The District Officer and Sheikh Ahmed met us at the quay, and we gave Shaheem the letter from Sheikh Alameen, asking him to accord us use of a stone house. They took us to one of the rooms adjacent to the garage which stood vacant. The room to the left of the garage was used by the Locust Control, and was stacked with locust bait. Lionel and myself brushed the place out while Shaheem arranged to have our luggage delivered. Shaheem went out of his way to help us: he even arranged for meals to be brought over to us, for several days running, until we were settled in.

We slept on the shaded veranda of the school building, on our camp beds. The garage room was our living room, kitchen, storeroom and clinic all rolled in one. We had brought some essential furniture items, such as tables, chairs and cupboards along with us.

Water posed a major problem. This was brought by women, usually twice a day, morning and evening, in goatskins. They had to walk the one and a half miles to the mainland and back, for just one bag. They would dig or scrape a hole in a dry wadi until muddy water oozed into the hole, forming a pool. Then, using a small tin can, they would transfer the water into the skin, filling it to the brim, and tie it at the neck. Arriving at our house, they would pour the water into our aluminium basin. It was just brown muddy water. We had to let it settle for half an hour before decanting it, leaving about a quarter of an inch of mud at the bottom of the bowl. We paid $1 Ethiopian (the equivalent of three shillings) for each bag. Normally one could purchase as many skins as one could afford. However, we arrived eleven days into the month of Ramadhan, with seventeen days still remaining. During this month, the women would only bring one skin a day, in the morning. This one skin per day, during Ramadhan, had to suffice for three of us (Lionel, myself and the houseboy), for drinking, cooking, medical work, shaving and toothbrushing. I put a tumblerful aside each day for washing clothes. We did not have the luxury of a refrigerator, but for drinking-water we filled a special canvas bag, added twelve Hallozone tablets against bowel diseases, and hung it up by a hook. Evaporation at the moist outer surface cooled it appreciably. We washed ourselves and any dishes or cooking utensils in the sea, using soap suitable for salt water.

The morning after our arrival, the clinic opened to welcome our first eleven patients. Sheikh Yassein was away in Asmara, but he had sent a message to a nephew, Abdu Hussein, aged 15, to offer us his services as a houseboy. After trying him out for one day we engaged him. I heard from Lionel sometime later that he had come to faith in the Lord Jesus. Later still, I heard that he had died, but never learnt of the circumstances of his untimely death.

Just two days after we arrived, the Quardhy, Sheikh Gamal Addeen, together with the Assistant Quardhy, Sheikh Ali, and several others, dropped by in the early evening. They were extremely affable and the Quardhy expressed his pleasure at our presence in Thio. It transpired that the Quardhy was the brother of the sorcerer in 'Edd, whose manner stood in stark contrast to Quardhy's upright and friendly character.

Despite such a smooth start, we apprehended that evening a counter-attack on the part of Satan, an attempt to discredit and evict us, or, at least, hinder our witness. We prayed specifically for the Lord to foil this plan and, further, to make us a fully integrated and vital part of the community. It was heart-warming to see the Lord graciously answering this petition in a number of ways.

The following day, Uccud, one of those who had visited us with the Quardhy, brought the latter's radio and asked if I could repair it. I did not have any radio-testing equipment but, with the light-bulb of my torch, I found that the seven and a half volt section of his battery was dead, but all the one and a half volt cells of the high-tension battery were alive. I had a small soldering iron, and with the Primus, I managed to make connections to provide seven and a half volts for the low-tension supply. The radio then worked well, and I heard that the Quardhy was delighted. The next day he sent over a large water-melon by way of thanks.

Just before I left Aden, my dear brother in Christ, Marouf, gave me his violin. He loved the violin, and could play impressively well, whereas my skill was limited to the rudiments I had acquired during six months violin lessons, as a boy of fourteen. The violin is a truly wonderful instrument in the hands of a master, but in the hands of a novice it becomes an instrument of torture, by which one can inflict untold pain on listeners' ears.

During the morning of our first Sunday in Thio, a crowd of children came over to visit us. I took out the violin, and started to play some Arabic gospel songs, teaching the children the words and tunes. One of these was, 'I was a prisoner of sin, ... but he bought me!' The children quickly picked them up and, through them, word spread that I was a musician! A number of times people would come, including Sheikh Ahmed and Sheikh Ali, and ask me to play them a tune. My rendering was absolutely awful, yet they maintained that it sounded great, just like on the radio!

Islamic Resistance

However, the counter-attack came very soon. On Tuesday, 1st May, we were invited to the house of Sheikh Ali, the Assistant Quardhy. Yassein, the customs officer, was there, as well as Ibrahim, the chief of the port, who was an Arab from Hadhramaut. During the course of the conversation, Ali turned to

Lionel and asked, 'Who is Jesus Christ?' There was no equivocation with Lionel. He would never go anywhere under false colours. He replied, 'Jesus Christ is the Son of God, and he died on the cross for my sins, and for yours, if you will accept him.' Both these tenets are strongly rejected by Islam. The reaction was accordingly hostile and it was like a door of acceptance slamming shut.

Later, Yassein, the customs officer, took us to one side. He was visibly outraged and lambasted Lionel in no uncertain terms, 'What? You come here to Thio and speak about such matters, of all things, in Ramadhan, when our religious zeal is at its peak.'

For the next couple of days, hardly a soul showed up at the clinic. The District Officer came over and asked how many patients we were getting. Lionel had been examining and treating patients from 8 am until about noon or 2 pm each day, but now almost nobody came.

The Lord overrules the boycott

Yassein was brought to us on an improvised stretcher. He was extremely sick. Lionel diagnosed his condition as acute appendicitis. We could not possibly consider operating on him in our circumstances, but if the appendix was to burst he would be finished. Lionel fitted the bars of his own camp bed into a kind of 'Fowler' position for him. He literally fought for the young man's life, acting both as doctor and nurse. He gave him everything he could to get him over the acute stage.

The boy knew that Lionel loved him, and was

fighting not only for his life, but for his eternal life also. His resentment and resistance just melted away. He whispered, 'I know God is dealing with me, I know that I have done wrong. Please pray for me.' After four days he came through. With his temperature back to normal, and able to eat again, we let him go home. Lionel recommended that I accompany him on the next Government boat to Massawa, where he should have his appendix removed by a surgeon, as he had a history of a grumbling appendix.

Eventually, sheer necessity brought the sick along to the clinic and soon everything was back in full swing. Sheikh Ali asked Lionel if he would see his wife, and barriers were broken down there. Sheikh Shaheem was taken ill, but after a few days on streptomycin he was back on his feet and most grateful. He admitted that he and the people were glad after all that we had come. Another villager, Omer, remarked that people were praising God that we had come. I responded that nothing could please me more than to hear that people were praising God on account of us.

Medical assistance was not the only way God used us to bless them. Abdu was our reliable liaison for purchasing food and other essentials. One morning, he turned up very late, looking as if he hadn't slept all night. I realized why when I noticed a bug crawling across his chest. From our unpleasant experience in Aden we had learned how to control a bug infestation, and had foresightedly brought 10kg of Gammexene with us.

I told Abdu that I would treat his bed so that he

could get a good night's sleep in future. I also offered to treat all the beds in Sheikh Yassein's compound, if they wished. They were rather reluctant when I began applying the product, but after three days' benefit from the measure they were delighted; all had enjoyed more restful sleep. As a result, Sheik Yassein's cousin asked me to treat all the beds on their compound. My next client was Sheikh Ahmed, creating a snowball-effect. I was summoned to numerous houses, leaving a trail of satisfied customers behind me.

A further means by which the Lord enabled me to win a place in peoples' hearts was watch-mending. I had dabbled in a little as a hobby, and had brought some watch-mending tools with me. In no time, I became honorary watch-mender of Thio. The Lord was indeed making us an essential part of the community.

After our first clash with Islamic power, even before the clinic started to pick up again, a man from Badda implored Lionel to come and treat the many sick there. Badda is an oasis, a few days' camel journey inland, with an abundance of water and, hence, a permanent settlement of about a thousand Danakil. The man offered to bring a string of camels to take us there. It was thus that the Lord, through love and concern for the people, succeeded in breaking down the barriers of opposition and prejudice.

It was a wonderful experience, and a tremendous privilege to take the gospel and the Word of God to a people to whom it had never before been preached before. Shaheem, Tilenty and others just gasped in astonishment when I told them of the wisdom that

God gave Solomon; how this enabled him to discern the truth in judgment, when he commanded the disputed baby to be cut in half. Similarly, parables, such as the 'Prodigal Son', really gripped them, as did modern accounts of lives transformed by the Lord Jesus.

I told them of those who, as the result of Lionel's visits, had come to know the Lord Jesus in the condemned cell in the Addis Ababa prison. It was a picture to see amazement written all over their faces, especially Tillenty's. He knew the prison situation all too well, and could never have imagined that someone might thank God for placing them there. A number of them expressed the desire to have the Bible or the New Testament in Arabic, a wish with which we happily complied. Among these hopefuls was the Quardhy, who became sincerely friendly and open. He showed a real appreciation of Christian truths.

A sumptuous Muslim feast marked the end of the Ramadhan fasting period. The children, boys and girls, clothed in festive attire, performed dances, as did the younger men. The latter's sequences combined elements of paganism, tribal customs and Islam.

On Monday, 21st May, the *Sabeto* arrived. Sheikh Yassein was aboard, returning from Asmara. He was delighted that we had arrived and had settled in well. He asked how things stood with respect to the school's project, and we told him frankly that it would depend on the local people. He said confidently, 'Don't worry, you will get your schools.'

I was to accompany Yassein to Massawa on the *Sabeto*, when it returned from Assab, in order to give him moral support during his appendix operation at the hospital. Travelling via Asmara, with the purpose of collecting my belongings, I was then to make my way to Aden, where Elna and I were to be married. After the wedding we were to go on furlough. This would be my first furlough after five and a half years on the field. It was agreed, however, that, during that time, I would do a few months' deputation work for the team in Britain. Barring the eventuality of the Lord opening the door to Israel, we were to return to Eritrea for the Danakil work. By way of replacement, Peter was to join Lionel in Thio, taking the next Government boat.

The *Sabeto* docked in on 25th May. There was a rush to get things ready and say all my goodbyes. Dear Lionel and I were both quite moved. He thanked me for the precious years I had been with him. I assured him the feeling was mutual.

The shared passage enabled Yassein and I to talk extensively. He was so open to my sharing with him the precious things of God, and so grateful too. He asked for a New Testament, and I gave him one in Tigrinia, his first language.

Asmara

When Peter opened the door to me at the headquarters his surprise was manifest. Later, when Jack[1] and

---

1. On June 9th, Kath Budd arrived from Aden to join Jack. She was thrilled with the house, and with Asmara. Asmara is indeed a beautiful garden city, about 6-7,000

Bruno returned, they rang for Marion to come up to Asmara. They were all eager to hear how the opening of our first Red Sea Mission Team Station in the Danakil had fared. Together, we had a good deal to praise the Lord for.

I went with Peter to see Ato Samuel. He gave Peter a three-month's extension to his tourist visa on the spot. We called on Ato Mubrahto, Director General of the Ministry of Health, and he was very pleased to hear of our reception in Thio.

Ato Qumulatchu, too, was delighted to hear the news of our reception in Danakil. He said that he would grant residents' visas to Enid Parker and Dorothy Davies, asking Jack to submit written applications, which he would then immediately authorize. Enid, a teacher, had already gone to Aden, and was simply waiting to be able to join Marion in Eritrea. They would work together in the Danakil.

Amongst the mail awaiting me in Asmara was a letter from Dr. Bernard Walker, postmarked Tiberias, Israel. He and his wife Karen sent their warmest congratulations on our forthcoming marriage. Knowing my call to Israel, he wrote that, if I believed it was of the Lord, the door was still open for me to come to Tiberias; this time, of course, with Elna.

I decided that it was best for me to travel to Aden via Thio, to settle this with Lionel, as it concerned him as much as me.

---

feet in altitude and enjoying a genial climate. This was a most agreeable change for her, after the heat and dust of Aden.

Lionel's blessing on my call to Israel

Peter and I bid our friends farewell and left for Massawa on the *Sabeto* on 19th June. We dropped anchor at Thio the same day. When dear Lionel came aboard I showed him Bernard's letter. He read it through, then his head sank on his chest. Slowly, he raised his head and said, 'I cannot say that you are letting me down now, Bev. I do believe it is of the Lord. The Lord bless you.' We were both choked with emotion, so preferred to simply embrace.

Elna and I still had to be accepted by the Church of Scotland Jewish Mission Committee, but I knew that the Lord was calling me to his land, to his people, as he had shown me shortly after my conversion. I recalled again with wonder how he had assured me that South Arabia would be the door by which I would enter Israel, an idea that to many had seemed inconceivable.

Of course, my move to Israel meant parting with my beloved friends. How I thanked God for those precious splendid years with them, and the manifestation of his presence among us.

Chapter 14

For Elna and I – Danakil or Israel?

Enid Parker

I arrived in Aden from Djibouti[1] on Monday morning, 2nd July, 1956 and was invited to lunch at the school. Until then, Elna and I had only managed to snatch a few minutes together, as she was busy teaching.

Twelve months previously a monthly allowance of £10 had been introduced for team members. As from our marriage, Elna also was to receive this, as an accepted member of the Team.

I had no bank account and very little money, nor had Elna been able to save anything of her meagre mission allowance. The Team had undertaken to pay my fare home, but Elna's fare presented us with a problem. She had committed herself to the Danish Mission for a term of six years. Nevertheless, in the case of marriage, one could be released from one's

---

1. This was the first opportunity I had of meeting Enid Parker. She had joined the Team and was preparing to go with Marion to the Danakil as a teacher. At the time of writing, she has only recently retired. She completed in full the transcription of the Danakil language and compiled the first ever Danakil dictionary and other materials. With a Danakil informant she has also produced much gospel audio-material for broadcasting. Her former co-worker in Djibouti, Yvonne Genat, has effected the first Afar (Danakil) translation of the New Testament.

contract. Moreover, Elna had given them eighteen months notice, to enable them to find and prepare her replacement. According to their regulations, as Elna had only served three years, she would be liable for half of their expenditure in sending her successor to Britain for English and to Lebanon for Arabic studies.

They were very fair. They demanded no refund, but rather offered to pay Elna's fare home if we were married in Denmark, as she would still be regarded as part of the Danish Mission. We considered the offer prayerfully, but were sure that we should be married in Aden where we both had many friends. Also, we felt it would be much better to travel home as man and wife.

We had to quickly book a berth on a ship. This was a step in faith as we had nowhere near enough money to pay the fare, let alone additional travelling expenses, such as the train fare from Marseilles to Denmark. However, the Lord gave us real peace of heart, and neither of us let anyone else know of our need.

We still had to get many other items too: wedding rings, suit cases, clothes, shoes and so on. I did not have a suit to my name, only tropical shorts and shirts. Lionel announced that I was to be fitted out with a wedding suit at his expense. Although it was the middle of the hot season, I ordered a warm woollen lounge suit. It would be a necessity in Europe, but in Aden, on our wedding day, it was like being boiled alive.

We certainly can testify wholeheartedly to the faithfulness of our beloved Lord: when the time came to settle the outstanding amount for our crossing we had the money in hand. This was thanks to a gentle trickle of continuous gifts, small and large, mostly anonymous. When we arrived in Denmark we still had about £100 in our pockets. To be sure, God tests our faith sometimes severely. Yet his purpose is by no means to crush it, rather, it is to strengthen it.

Our wedding was held in the Danish Mission Church on 14th July, 1956, with the Danish minister, Rev. Erik Stidsen, officiating. Dr. Kristine Carlsen gave the bride away, and Bruno was the best man. Elna's headmistress, Grethe Jensen, arranged for the reception to be held on the school premises. The church was full, the ceremony and ensuing celebrations a success (with the exception of the suit)!

That evening, Elna suggested that we read our Bible together, continuing from the passage where I had left off in my own Quiet Time. That was Jeremiah 32, so we started on chapter 33 together. It was such a surprise, and tremendous joy, when we reached verses 10-11, which read: '... shall be heard ... in the cities of Judah, and in the streets of Jerusalem, the voice of the bridegroom, and the voice of the bride, the voice of them that shall say, Praise the LORD of hosts: for the LORD is good.' We know that God's Word cannot be reduced to or applied willy-nilly to any individual circumstances, yet we were sure that it was no coincidence that we had read that particular passage that evening.

A special reception

We were invited by many of our dear friends to their homes for meals, and happy fellowship.

One of the highlights was a reception arranged for us by the young church, and held in Dr. Affara's house. The calling into existence of this band of disciples was truly a miracle wrought by God's Grace. We still treasure, and indeed use, the lovely canteen of cutlery, which they presented to us on that occasion.

The boat was scheduled to leave on Sunday morning, 22nd July, and many of our dear friends and colleagues came aboard to bid us farewell. On board, we met some other missionaries; together we arranged to hold daily Bible studies. These meetings went very well, and were well attended.

The trip up the Red Sea and through the Suez Canal was most enjoyable. On 26th July, 1956 we arrived at Port Said, and after four hours ashore, we returned to the ship, which promptly sailed out into the Mediterranean, *en route* for Marseilles. It was only when we arrived in Marseilles on 30th July that we heard that President Nasser had nationalized the Suez Canal at 7 am on the 27th July, the morning after we left Port Said. Consequently, the canal was closed to shipping for months. It would have been a dreadful state of affairs if we had been barred entry into the canal or, even worse, if we had been trapped in it. Naturally, our praise of our merciful God was effusive.

We arrived at Elna's home in Denmark on 1st August to a tremendous welcome. Many family members had assembled for the occasion and that evening a grand supper was laid on. The time in Denmark seemed to fly by, swallowed up as it was by addressing congregations, taking meetings, showing slides, meeting friends and family in various parts of Denmark, and lending a hand on Elna's parents' farm.

On 14th September, I left for Britain to do deputation work for the Team, while Elna stayed on in Denmark. The following evening, I arrived at the 'team headquarters': this was Gypsie's modest bedsitting room – rented in a Christian Guest House in Parkstone, Dorset – which she shared with her octogenarian mother. The room was chock-a-block, chiefly with material related to the Team. Arrangements were made for me to stay at the Guest House. I then set off on a series of deputation meetings, arranged by Gypsie.

Edinburgh and the Church of Scotland

In early October, business took me to Edinburgh where I was warmly received by Mrs Walker and the children. They were back in Scotland on account of the children's education.

Rev. Clephane McCanna, Secretary of the Church of Scotland Jewish Mission Committee, informed me that I was to appear before the Appointments Subcommittee, at noon on 11th October. Dr. Affara and Lionel had penned two highly recommendatory testimonials, which I handed to Mr. McCanna.

Approximately seventy members from all over Scotland had assembled for the meeting. During the interview, it emerged that I had been christened as an infant, but had been baptized by immersion after coming to know the Lord Jesus as my Saviour. I hastened to add, however, that I knew many true believers whose opinions on baptism differed from mine, but refused to let this impair my fellowship with them. This qualification appeared to inspire murmurs of approval.

An elderly minister then addressed me for a while. He told me that I was going out to a very difficult field, and that I was not to speak to people about my faith. My work should be carried out conscientiously and to the highest standard, thereby allowing my conduct and integrity to express my faith. As he continued in this fashion, I was sure that I could not accept an appointment on those terms, although I did accept, of course, that in witnessing we must seek the Lord's leading and demonstrate discernment.

There was deadly silence for some time. Then one of the committee members rose to his feet and asked me what my purpose was in wanting to go to Israel. This question afforded me the opportunity I had been waiting for. I replied, 'I understand that my foremost duty will be responsibility for the maintenance work of the hospital under Dr. Bernard Walker. However, my chief purpose in wanting to go to Israel is to take the gospel of the Lord Jesus Christ to the Jewish people.' This evidently hit a chord amongst those assembled. Murmurs of assent rippled across the room. I was greatly encouraged. If I were to be accepted it would certainly not be under false pretences.

Mr. McCanna then escorted me to a waiting room, and said that he would inform me of the committee's decision in due course. After fifteen minutes he returned to announce that I had been unanimously accepted. Truly, 'he openeth and no man closeth' (Rev. 3:7). Mr. McCanna said they would proceed to make visa applications for us.

On the 20th October, I received a letter from Elna saying that she was not sure, but it was possible that our first-born was on the way. If this was indeed the case, delivery was expected about June 1957. I was enthralled by the news.

The Israeli-Egyptian War

On 29th October, at 5 am, the Israeli army invaded Sinai and was pressing on towards the Suez Canal. On 30th October, the France-British attack on Egypt hit the headlines. A full-scale war was developing.

I took an overnight bus to London and on 1st November went to Harwich to meet Elna. She confirmed that the little one was definitely on the way. We talked about the present political climate in the Middle East and our call to Israel. Elna held fast to the conviction that God was calling us there and expressed her willingness to obey, should our visas materialize, in spite of the war. I was deeply grateful to the Lord for giving me such a wife. With an eased conscience, I wrote to Mr. McCanna to the effect that we were convinced our place was in Israel and were undeterred by the threat of war.

The war was brought to a close within about a week. Due to a delay with the visas and other formalities, we were unable to leave before 2nd January, 1957. However, we were glad that the Lord had put our willingness to the test, as our strengthened resolve and assurance of his call was consequently able to withstand subsequent trials.

During our wait, Elna stayed with Mrs. Walker, while I did some more deputation work for the Team.

I met a number of the young RAF men who had surrendered their lives to the Lord when he had moved amongst them in power in Aden. It was a cause of heartfelt thankfulness to the Lord to hear how they were being trained and prepared for the Lord's purposes. Ron Harbottle was training to be a teacher, with a view to joining the Team. He arranged for me to speak at the college, and his father arranged further meetings for me in the Newcastle and Gateshead area, pending my return to Edinburgh.

The Annual Team Meeting
This was held in London on 6th December and registered a high attendance. The two main speakers were Rev. Leith Samuel and Prof. J.N.D. Anderson. I was able to show slides, illustrating the history and development of the Team and what God had achieved through it. It was quite a bombshell when I announced that we had been accepted for Israel by the Church of Scotland, and would be leaving the Team. I went on to express how grateful I was for the precious years the Lord had given me whilst a part of it. The response was one of love and understanding. Indeed, some shared my burden for Israel.

Leaving the Team; Departure for Israel

On 21st December, 1956, I returned to Edinburgh. As our visas had come through, we were preparing to leave by plane from Prestwick on 2nd January, 1957. I had learnt much as a member of the team: I had become more firmly rooted in the Word of God; I had grown as a consequence of having to actively place my trust in it; and I had gained a greater understanding of the function and beauty of Christ's body.

For some time, I could not appreciate why the Lord should train me in an Arab Muslim setting. Now I realize that in order to communicate effectively with the Jewish people it is essential to understand the environment in which they live, that is a Muslim culture, with Arab Muslim neighbours.

Work in Israel

My 'tent making' consisted in working as a hospital engineer for five and a half years at the Church of Scotland Hospital in Tiberias, and also as secretary and treasurer during the change-over period before it officially became a hospice. Our three boys were all born in Tiberias. I seized every opportunity that presented itself to tell others – especially Jews – of what God had done to redeem lost men and women, Jew and Gentile, offering the wonderful hope of eternal life to those who respond.

I was invited to join the Edinburgh Medical Hospital in Nazareth for one year. Elna found considerable demand for maths tutoring among student nurses. She also became involved in holding

Bible studies and organizing outings for the girls. I was expecting the Lord to move me to a more Jewish work environment, but I was there for fifteen years until retirement.

Later, our eldest son John became very active in the Christian Union whilst studying Archaeology at Edinburgh University. In 1983, he was commissioned by the International Federation of Evangelical Students (IFES) to pioneer Christian student unions in Israel – a move that was evidently prompted by God. Praise the Lord! The fruit of that work is none other than a mature indigenous movement of Jewish and Arab students. The Government have even granted them the status of a non-profit making society, with the freedom to practice and propagate their own religion, and to distribute Bibles, New Testaments and other Christian literature.

In 1988, at the IFES four-yearly General Committee, held in Columbia, the movement was accepted as a member of the International Movement, IFES. This is a very strategic work. It represents the arm of the Church in the academic world. It is most important that some of the future statesmen and church leaders experience oneness in Christ on an international and interdenominational basis. The movement benefits Christian students too, providing a medium for fellowship and mutual edification in a spiritually hostile environment.

It was only after seeing what the Lord was accomplishing through John that I could fully appreciate the value of those years in Nazareth in preparing John for the role the Lord had assigned him.

During his primary and secondary education in Upper Nazareth, he had attended Jewish schools, learning Hebrew and Arabic, alongside his many Jewish friends. At the hospital – which was international and interdenominational – he made many Arab friends. As a result, he was fluent in English, Arabic and Hebrew. I then understood this was one of the main reasons for which the Lord had kept us in Nazareth for so long. Indeed, I apologized to the Lord for my impatience and lack of faith and acknowledged that he knows his business.

I had obtained an Israeli patent for an apparatus which produced highly pure pyrogen free distilled water from the crude steam of the hospital laundry boiler. The hospital superintendent, Dr. Bernath, and myself were considering launching a business enterprise to develop the patent. At the same time a Danish nurse, who was a friend of Elna, was retiring to Denmark and wanted to sell her 1969 VW Beetle. With the lump sum awarded me by the hospital on retirement, I purchased the car as I thought it would serve our business purposes. The company never materialized, but the Lord had a better use for the car.

Bible Distribution to the Kibbutzim

After retiring from the hospital, we were clearly led to Haifa. Rose Warmer, a Hungarian Jewess, was a resident in Ebenezer, a Christian retirement home in Haifa. She had come to faith in the Lord Jesus just before the Nazis invaded Hungary. Together with the other Jews she was taken to Aushwitz, then to Essen as a slave labourer. They were sent to Bergen Belsen, to die by starvation and disease, just two weeks before it was liberated by British troops. Four days before liberation, she found she had typhus and was near to death for three months. She had been very conscious of God's presence with her through it all, and was so grateful that she gave him her life for his purposes.

The Lord showed that he wanted her to go to Israel to distribute his Word widely, in Hebrew and other languages, without charge. Amazingly the Lord enabled her to do this. In the late 1970s she had some severe heart attacks and was admitted into Ebenezer. For a few years, a pastor did the distribution work until he died of a heart attack. For some time, Rose was deeply concerned, she was receiving money to buy Bibles, but had no one to distribute them.

I had known her for over twenty years and she knew that I loved the Lord and his Word. I was asking the Lord for an outlet of service, and was sure it was of him when Rose asked me to take on the Bible distribution work, saying she would supply the Bibles. She was delighted when she knew that I had a car, and she came with me for two weeks to ensure that I could do the work to her satisfaction. The work had developed to that of distribution to Kibbutzim throughout the country, visiting almost every Kibbutz once a year, or year and a half.

In 1983 it was found I had chronic lymphatic leukaemia with haemolysis, my haemoglobin had fallen to 5.1 (normal 12.5). The Lord laid it on a dear Jewish believer to leave his work as an analytical chemist and take over the Bible work so that it would not cease. The Lord restored me to health and strength, although I still most definitely have leukaemia, but do not need medication. Up to the time of writing we are able to go together, a believing Jew and a believing Gentile, one in heart and Spirit. In so many ways my sickness has been a great blessing.

Ongoing discipleship

This last few years the Lord has drawn me into a much deeper relationship with himself. He has opened my ear, much in line with Isaiah 50:4. Kneeling at his feet in the early morning leads to precious fellowship, two way rather than monologue, as it mostly was. The vital nature of discipleship has become startlingly clear as he has been showing me various issues from his viewpoint rather than my own, often vague, confused and conflicting understanding.

In the Lord's School with the Team, the Lord had showed me more deeply the meaning and importance of discipleship. He also showed me the enormous task he longs to perform through his church in every generation. Yet the proportion of labourers is very meagre and the necessary support is very scanty. Those who do respond, in going, giving and praying, are very precious to him.

Christ's great commission to his church is not only to bring sinners of all nations to repentance and redemption through his blood, but also includes the vital goal of making them *all* disciples of Christ. This is vital for the extension of God's Kingdom. Discipleship is not an optional extra. It is most important for Christians to realize that they cannot make disciples of others unless they are disciples themselves.

The Lord has been making it clearer to me what true discipleship really is. In Matthew 11:28-30, the Lord gives two invitations. The first is, 'Come unto me.' He invites, but we must respond by coming to him personally. Who can come to him? These verses invite those who are desperately striving to earn their salvation by good works, as well as those who have a terrible load of sin on them. Of course, Christ's invitation is given to everyone, but it is only when we are convicted by the Holy Spirit that we realize our need and respond to Jesus. When we do respond, true to his promise, Jesus takes our load away. What rest we then discover! This rest is free, it does not depend on any of our attempts to pay for our sin, but only on what he has done for us.

But that is only the beginning of the Christian life. Jesus longs for each of his disciples to enter into a much closer relationship with himself. We have this experience by responding to his second invitation to take his yoke upon us and learn *from* him as his disciples. What is the yoke he wants us to share with him? It is to be wholeheartedly yielded to him, in a way that he can accept. No-one should shrink from this, for as he says, 'my yoke is easy and my burden is light.' This offering must be once and for all, and unconditional. When we take his yoke on us, it is no longer merely us doing things for him, which in eternal terms is ineffective. Rather it is him preparing us to accompany him, in our yielded bodies, to effectively accomplish the role God has for us.

He shows us how we can have the tremendous privilege of him using us to bring great glory to God and to extend his Kingdom as his instruments in bringing great blessing and salvation to lost sinners.

We should all earnestly pray for the Lord to grant an outpouring of his Holy Spirit. That is our greatest need. May he grant conviction, cleansing, renewal, consecration, commissioning, empowering and directing so that his redeemed people will fulfil his purposes in a way satisfying to his great heart of love.

I do thank the Lord from my heart for taking me through a school of his choice, in the Backside of the Desert, with what was developing into the Red Sea Mission Team. It was God's 'Grain of Mustard Seed' in them that had such potential.

Epilogue

'Verily, verily, I say unto you, Except a corn of wheat fall into the ground and die, it abideth alone, but if it die, it bringeth forth much fruit' (John 12:24).

The instrument God used to found the Red Sea Team, Dr. Lionel Gurney, went to be with his beloved Lord on February 18th, 1995, at the age of 84.

Lionel was brought up in a godly home. He knew biblical truths well, such as Christ dying on the cross for our sins, and accepted them mentally. However, he joined a live youth movement and it was there the Lord brought home these truths in a living, personal way. He responded by embracing God's promises by faith, and had the assurance that he was redeemed, that all his sins had been forgiven, paid for by the blood of the Lord Jesus.

In due course he studied medicine at Bristol University and became very interested in surgery as his career. However, the Lord Jesus had a plan for his life, and challenged Lionel to be one of his disciples, to take his yoke upon himself, and to be taught and led of him. Lionel realized this had to be an unconditional surrender to his Lord, and responded wholeheartedly. That was when Lionel died – when he accepted self to be crucified.

I trust this book has given a glimpse of the Lord Jesus at work, in and through one he called to be his disciple, and by whom he called out many other disciples.

Reaching For The Crescent Moon

The story of Michael and Mary Cawthorne as told by Helena Rogers

ISBN 1 857 92 123 2   pocket paperback   272 pages

Not many people have the opportunity to visit Pakistan. Fewer still have the pleasure of viewing the Khyber Pass, and far smaller in number are those blessed folk who have travelled through the Khyber Pass to the ancient land of Afghanistan.

Mary and Mike Cawthorne are numbered in that blessed few. Their home in Pakistan at times served as a refuge for some of the lost souls my wife and I were reaching out to in Afghanistan. Michael and Mary visited us when they came to Afghanistan, and their presence always brought joy and encouragement.

This book will take you back over many years to visit with Michael and Mary as they journey to the land of Pakistan. You will walk with them in the market places and the bazaars, and your heart will join with theirs as they reach for the crescent moon, and the people who live in the shadow of that crescent.

I commend this book because it is about two of God's servants who gave their lives on the front lines for Jesus.

Floyd McClung
International Director, Youth With a Mission

Rescue Shop Within a Yard of Hell
Stewart Dinnen
ISBN 1 85792 1224   pocket paperback   272 pages

The remarkable story of evangelism by Betel among the drug addicts and AIDs sufferers in Spain. In addition to the strategies of the workers being explained, there are testimonies from converted addicts, some of whom became leaders in the church.

Faith on Fire
Norman Grubb and the building of WEC
Stewart Dinnen
ISBN 185792 3219   large format   240 pages

Norman Grubb 'inherited' the leadership of WEC from his father-in-law, C. T. Studd. Leslie Brierley said of Grubb, 'To experience his dynamic leadership ... was my unforgettable experience.'

A Hundred Houses
The story of Joe and Irene Rowley who work in Brazil with Unevangelised Fields Mission
ISBN 1 871 676 77 0 pocket paperback 160 pages

Life as a missionary is often seen as romantic, but Irene Rowley tells of the reality – coping with disease, misunderstanding, a handicapped child and home-sickness. Yet her determination to work for God in Brazil carries her through and gives purpose to all that she does. David Waite writes: 'People will be challenged after reading this down-to-earth, honest book. We learn of the tensions of the missionary life, the heat, dust and squalor, and of some of the problems of the people. It is refreshingly different.'

60 Great Founders
Geoffrey Hanks
ISBN 1 85792 1402 large format 496 pages

This book details the Christian origins of 60 organizations, most of which are still committed to the God-given, world-changing vision with which they began. Among them are several mission organizations.

70 Great Christians
Geoffrey Hanks
ISBN 1 871 676 800 large format 352 pages

The author surveys the growth of Christianity throughout the world through the lives of prominent individuals who were dedicated to spreading the faith. Two sections of his book are concerned with mission; one section looks at the nineteenth century missionary movement, and the other details mission growth throughout the twentieth century.

Mission of Discovery
ISBN 1 85792 2581 large format 448 pages

The fascinating journal of Robert Murray McCheyne's and Andrew Bonar's journeys throughout Palestine and Europe in the 1840s to investigate if the Church of Scotland should set up a mission to evangelise the Jewish people. From their investigation, much modern Jewish evangelism has developed.